Leslie Leyland Fields was not only n
mentor me with the way she actually
unforgettable story that gives sojourners hope—and gives God all the glory. She is
a profoundly wise, Christ-formed guide whose every word I will always read.

ANN VOSKAMP, *New York Times* bestselling author

When I first began writing, Leslie quickly became a trusted voice. Not simply on
the art of writing but on the living, breathing act of writing. It's hard enough to
use good verbs and precise language, but that's not the hardest part. The ghosts of
our stories, the self-doubt, and the fear—those are the parts of the writing journey
we all need a hand holding ours through. Leslie offers that critical companionship
and inspires by example of what can happen when we learn to tell our stories.

LIZ DITTY, author of *God's Many Voices*

Leslie has a deep commitment to writing life-giving words. She crafts them
beautifully and helps others do likewise. This book promises to prompt the best
out of storytellers and creatives.

MAX LUCADO, *New York Times* bestselling author

This inspired writing warrior has plunged deep into her well of talent to teach
a vital lesson: We don't own our stories. God writes them on our lives, then
appoints us to stand up and share them. It's time to heed this truth and act. An
impassioned Leslie Leyland Fields dares to show us how.

PATRICIA RAYBON, award-winning author of *My First White Friend* and *I Told the Mountain to Move*

A magical, moving, and essential book for anyone who wants to understand why
their story matters and to write that story! Leslie Leyland Fields tells her story
while helping others tell their stories, all while creating an extraordinary story of
writing itself. Personal and profound, inspirational and practical, God-focused and
with its feet firmly placed on the ground, this is a necessary and beautiful book for
anyone and everyone because we've all been blessed with the story we have—and
that story is worth our telling.

BRET LOTT, *New York Times* bestselling author, director of MFA program at the College of
Charleston

Like many others, I've learned much about storytelling from Leslie. Leslie's many
stories, some heartbreaking and some glorious, do something an abstract proposition
can never do: They penetrate the hidden realities of the world in which we live, into

the barely known realities of our own life. Leslie will teach you how to find those hidden realities with texture and tone.

REV. CANON DR. SCOT MCKNIGHT, professor of New Testament at Northern Seminary

Whether you write because you seek meaning from your life's experiences, wish to pass on your story to family and friends, or dream of sharing a testimony of God's work in your life with a wider audience, veteran writer Leslie Leyland Fields believes that your story matters. This book is a lively, relatable, and gracious master class that will guide you step-by-step through mining the riches of your life's experiences, bringing the core events to the surface, and shaping those events into writing that will communicate the story only your life can tell. Loaded with examples, prompts, and warm insight, this beautiful book belongs in the hands of everyone who longs to find a way to communicate their story to others.

MICHELLE VAN LOON, author of *Becoming Sage*

If you are never blessed with the opportunity to take a writing class from Leslie Leyland Fields, then at least read this book. It's a work of four strands: why you can and should tell your life stories, clear teaching on how to do so (with helpful exercises and student examples), stories from her own life, and a useful tale of working with an agent and getting published—in short, the entire journey. All told with the wit and wisdom of someone who is doing the hard work right along with you.

DANIEL TAYLOR, author of *Tell Me a Story* and *Do We Not Bleed?*

The greatest power of Story is to illuminate. That's how Leslie Leyland Fields begins her own story—a vivid retelling of pivotal events in her own life and an encouragement to each of us to tell ours. Written in her own bright, conversational style, this fresh writing book is chockablock with lived experience that translates into guidelines for our own storytelling. The author's energy bleeds from the pages. Read this, come face to face with this woman of God, and hear her affirm, "You can do this, and here's how."

LUCI SHAW, author of *Thumbprint in the Clay* and (forthcoming) *The Generosity: New Poems*

Whether you consider yourself a writer or are just beginning to find your story, I cannot imagine a more inviting mentor than Leslie Leyland Fields. The book you hold in your hands will take you on a journey. I'm convinced you'll find your voice, and the tools to use it, along the way.

CATHERINE MCNIEL, author of *Long Days of Small Things* and *All Shall Be Well*

LESLIE LEYLAND FIELDS

YOUR STORY MATTERS

FINDING, WRITING, AND LIVING THE TRUTH OF YOUR LIFE

NavPress

A NavPress resource published in alliance
with Tyndale House Publishers

NavPress is the publishing ministry of The Navigators, an international Christian organization and leader in personal spiritual development. NavPress is committed to helping people grow spiritually and enjoy lives of meaning and hope through personal and group resources that are biblically rooted, culturally relevant, and highly practical.

For more information, visit NavPress.com.

Your Story Matters: Finding, Writing, and Living the Truth of Your Life

Copyright © 2020 by Leslie Leyland Fields. All rights reserved.

Visit the author at LeslieLeylandFields.com.

A NavPress resource published in alliance with Tyndale House Publishers.

NAVPRESS and the NavPress logo are registered trademarks of NavPress, The Navigators, Colorado Springs, CO. *TYNDALE* is a registered trademark of Tyndale House Publishers. Absence of ® in connection with marks of NavPress or other parties does not indicate an absence of registration of those marks.

The Team: Don Pape, Publisher; Caitlyn Carlson, Acquisitions Editor; Elizabeth Schroll, Copy Editor; Dean H. Renninger, Designer

Author photo by Jessica Davis Photography, copyright © 2016. All rights reserved.

Cover photograph of road copyright © Matt Smith/EyeEm/Getty Imagescopyright. All rights reserved.

Cover photograph of car by Sergio Souza on Unsplash.com.

The author is represented by the literary agency of WordServe Literary, www.wordserveliterary.com.

All Scripture quotations, unless otherwise indicated, are taken from the Holy Bible, *New International Version,*® *NIV.*® Copyright © 1973, 1978, 1984, 2011 by Biblica, Inc.® Used by permission. All rights reserved worldwide. Scripture quotations marked ESV are from the ESV® Bible (The Holy Bible, English Standard Version®), copyright © 2001 by Crossway, a publishing ministry of Good News Publishers. Used by permission. All rights reserved. Scripture quotations marked GNT are taken from the Good News Translation in Today's English Version, Second Edition, copyright © 1992 by American Bible Society. Used by permission. Scripture quotations marked RSV are taken from the Revised Standard Version of the Bible, copyright © 1952 [2nd edition, 1971] by the Division of Christian Education of the National Council of the Churches of Christ in the United States of America. Used by permission. All rights reserved. Scripture quotations marked BSB are taken from The Holy Bible, Berean Study Bible, BSB. Copyright © 2016, 2018 by Bible Hub. Used by permission. All rights reserved worldwide. Scripture quotations marked GW are taken from GOD'S WORD®, copyright 1995 by God's Word to the Nations. Used by permission of God's Word Mission Society. All rights reserved. Scripture quotations marked NKJV are taken from the New King James Version,® copyright © 1982 by Thomas Nelson, Inc. Used by permission. All rights reserved. Scripture quotations marked NLT are taken from the Holy Bible, New Living Translation, copyright © 1996, 2004, 2015 by Tyndale House Foundation. Used by permission of Tyndale House Publishers, Carol Stream, Illinois 60188. All rights reserved.

Some of the anecdotal illustrations in this book are true to life and are included with the permission of the persons involved. All other illustrations are composites of real situations, and any resemblance to people living or dead is purely coincidental.

For information about special discounts for bulk purchases, please contact Tyndale House Publishers at csresponse@tyndale.com, or call 1-800-323-9400.

ISBN 978-1-64158-219-3

Printed in the United States of America

26	25	24	23	22	21	20
7	6	5	4	3	2	1

For all who have dared to remember, to write, and to share
their own remarkable story,
and for all those just beginning.
Wherever two or three gather to write,
God is there.

CONTENTS

INTRODUCTION

*There is no greater agony than bearing
an untold story inside you.*

MAYA ANGELOU

I AM STANDING in front of a hundred women in a conference room in Ulaanbaatar, the capital of Mongolia, and I am not in good shape. I am jet-lagged after thirty-some hours of traveling. My brain is full of wool stuffing. My eyes are squinting, trying to peer through it. I am wearing black suede loafers, black slacks, and a burgundy blouse, but my clothes are not lending me any confidence today. I have taught in other countries through translators before, but I've never taught a writing seminar through a translator. And I know that everything I will say to these women will be utterly new; this is an oral culture, not a literary culture. Here, they believe that only important people write stories and books. I am nervous.

The women sit at desks with notebooks in front of them. I've met a few of them already at another seminar the night before: Oodmaa, Badmaa, Becca, Battsetseg, Erka. They range in age from nineteen to seventy-five, all with silken black hair, dark eyes, and busy, difficult lives. Some have driven in from the countryside, hours away. Some have come on early-morning buses. Some have braved the city traffic, a snarl of vehicles so dense that you're only allowed to drive certain days.

These women are sheepherders, pastors' wives, doctors,

university students, mothers, tour guides, accountants. One woman is a professional driver for the government; some of them were once nomads and just moved to the city. A few of their husbands once lived in the underground sewers, alcoholics trying to survive the Mongolian winters next to the warm water pipes under the city. And some of these women are pastors. One of them has started two churches, one in a yurt outside the city, where I would go to preach that Sunday.

They're enrolled in a two-year school of ministry. And today, they are here for a full day of instruction in writing and sharing their own stories.

Because I am so tired, I am in overdrive. I speak with passion, I raise my hands in the air, halting every sentence or two for Chinzurig, the translator, to speak. I hold my position and my expression while my words are translated. I've come all this way, and I have so much to give them! The women sit with heads bent, taking detailed notes. I hardly see their faces.

Suddenly the director of the school of ministry, who is sitting against the wall, jumps to her feet and interrupts me mid-sentence: "Leslie! Could you stop a minute?"

I startle. I've been interrupted before, even heckled (in Hollywood, while receiving an obscure award and giving thanks to God!), but not like this. I look at her askance, mentally putting my hands on my hips but trying to look unfazed, professional.

Janice smiles sweetly at me. "I'm sensing that the women here don't feel worthy to tell their stories. They don't feel like their stories matter. What can you say about that?"

I already spoke to this. Didn't Janice hear me? I turn impatiently and watch the women as Chinzurig speaks her words in Mongolian. They are looking at me with wide eyes, as if someone has just spilled their deepest secret and they wonder what I will do with it. I see it then. I see the doubt. I see the glaze over their eyes and their hands resting now from too many notes, too much information. I see them watching me as a white American woman, thinking of me as someone famous from a rich country far away, someone not at all like them.

My chest falls. Of course. They don't know who I am. I put down my notes, come out from behind the music stand that was my podium. I stand there before them with my arms hanging down. How do I tell them about this girl in the woods, one of six kids, who had nothing anyone wanted? I wore faded, home-made, hand-me-down dresses. I had four pairs of holey underwear to my name. Our food was doled out to our plates, and there was never any more. I had stringy hair because we washed our hair with soap—we couldn't afford shampoo. My classmates often made fun of my clothes and appearance. I've spent fifteen years of my life changing diapers. Every summer I live on a wilderness island in Alaska without flushing toilets or a shower. I am not rich, fancy, or important.

How much of this do I say?

I don't remember exactly what I said, but I ended like this: "I was a nobody searching for God, for something real and true. And God found me. He left the ninety-nine sheep and came out into the woods, climbed that mountain, and found me and carried me home. I am the hundredth sheep. And you are the hundredth sheep as well. We were all of us lost, wandering, and God found us."

"Tell me about that," I say to these women, who are now seeing me more clearly. "Tell me that story."

Every one of them—Oodmaa, Badmaa, Becca, Battsetseg, Erka, the grandma in the front row, the doctor in the back row, the Japanese pastor—their eyes are bright and wet, and in minutes their heads are bent and they are writing furiously. They do not stop, even when I ask them to.

I watch, breathing deeply, the wool in my head slowly dissolving. How did I forget? How did I forget in a class about writing stories to tell my own story? No matter what country we live in, no matter our neighborhood, our politics, our religion, our age, no matter even our shared pursuit of God, we risk passing like strange ships in the long night. Time, busyness, the speed of life will keep us apart unless we braid word around word from our own passage, then toss it out, coiled, shimmering, toward the hands on the other deck open, waiting to catch, to coil and secure the two ships together, hull to hull. Don't we all sail the same turbulent waters? Aren't we longing to stop for a while, to not be alone on the high seas?

I've been laying down one word after another now for most of my life. And have been teaching others to do the same for three decades. The process we'll enter in this book isn't about becoming a writer, though some of you will become writers through it. It's not about writing a bestseller, though that is also possible. No—this act of turning around to write into our lives is about recovering what's been lost and discovering all that's new. We know some of the truth of our story, but not all of it. Under our skin, a whirring, beating engine of a heart purrs and pumps us through our days, our years. And often we whirl so fast, our eyes are closed against the speed of it, the how of it, and especially the why of it. Every day we are different; the world awakens new, and the memories of what was and what we've been, and the discovery of who we are now, could all be lost. But we have this chance now to stop. We're stopping to ask the questions we did not know to ask. We're stopping to find the difficult and beautiful truths of our lives. And what a gift it will be, to send this awakening, these crafted and compelling words on to others, that they—and we—may not pilgrim alone.

That is what we'll do in the pages ahead. I'll lead you step-by-step in discovering and telling your own unique story—or someone else's. And by the end of this first step in your writing journey, you will see what I have seen: that there is no part of human experience not worthy of attention, illumination, and restoration.

I'll take you as well through the story of Story in my life and the unexpected ways writing into my life has changed my life. I was reminded that day in Ulaanbaatar that this process works best when we do it together. So as I invite your stories, I'll share some of mine as well. Some of them are brand-new stories that I've just discovered and recovered in the writing of this book. They're mostly happy stories, but there are a few crashes along the way, some hilarities, a few absurdities, and even a bit of tragedy and cautionary tale thrown in the mix. I want you to know I'm on this path of discovery with you.

What will happen as you work your way through these pages? I can tell you what I've seen again and again, in prisons, churches, living rooms, classrooms, conferences, around the US, in Mongolia, Canada, South Africa, Slovakia, France. Everyday people like you and me have discovered that writing the truest words we can find from our lives can order our chaotic present, help us make sense of a jumbled past, move us from grief to hope. Writing can bring healing to wounds; it can even open the door for reconciliation and forgiveness. Learning to tell a truer story will help us live a better story.

I know this sounds like overspeak. I know some of you are skeptics. After all, we live in an Age of Story, and the stories that saturate our culture are not always benign. Since the rise of postmodernism, many have traded belief in knowable objective Truths with belief in our own personal stories and truths. "Your truth" and "my truth" and "my story" can be assertions of our own unquestioned perceptions. More recently, Story has even been co-opted as a sales strategy. Every business, product, and entity—from the political candidate running for office, to the tire shop down the street, to the box of oatmeal on your breakfast table—regales you with their story using "story branding." So caution makes sense. But we can believe in the importance and power of personal stories without disavowing grander truths.

In fact, this is the greatest power of Story: to illuminate and reveal larger spiritual truths in ways that mere facts can't quite do. Even in decades past, when our culture subscribed to facts and the knowability of truth, God's Word still spoke mostly through story. This Age of Story is an opportunity, then, not a crisis. Few people are interested in theological arguments. Even fewer will listen to religious clichés. But they'll still listen to a good story well told. As a friend recently said, "Most of my children and my grand-children have walked away from the church. They won't listen to a sermon. But maybe they'll hear my story." Yes, I say to him, to you, to myself. Tell them a true story. Tell them a better story than they've heard.

Some of you are ready! Some of you are waiting impatiently to dive into the rhythm and rhyme of this process. You've adopted two special-needs children from Russia. You're a mother, alone, raising your daughter in a wheelchair. You're capturing your childhood on the Kansan prairie. You're walking with your son out of addiction. You're recovering your father's stories from Vietnam. Whatever your story is, you know it's waiting to find its shape and voice on the page.

Some of you have lived awhile, and your children and grand-children don't know half of your life. They don't know what you came from. They don't know what you endured, or the ways God showed up. Or the ways you think he didn't. (My father had only one story to tell of his time serving in the infantry in World War II. He was riding a tank in Germany. They stopped for a break. He perched on the outside of the tank while the others took shelter in a barn. Suddenly he had the distinct urge to get off the tank. As soon as he approached the barn, a shell exploded right where he had been sitting. "Don't you think maybe that was God who nudged you off the tank and saved you?" I asked my agnostic father. He shrugged. "Maybe.")

You want them to know because some of these events have touched them, too, though they don't know it. They haven't been ready to listen, or you haven't been able to say the words out loud. But you can write these words on the page. Or perhaps you are writing someone else's story. My friend Joy is writing her mother-in-law's story of living in France through World War II. Whether it's your own story or someone else's, you want to learn to craft a narrative that can belong to your whole family.

Maybe you have no idea what your "story" is, and you aren't sure you want to take the time to find out. I get it. I was almost forty when I began to write about my life, and I was barely able to describe the hundred coexistent pieces, let alone imagine a single story from their frayed ends. That summer, I wandered the vales of my Alaskan island, muttering to myself, "What *is* my story?" And you know, I found it. Or it found me. Those words turned an isolated island into home. They turned a victim into a survivor. Those words carved and shaped an identity and belonging I didn't know was mine to claim. My story was both harder and better than I knew. Yours will be the same.

Some of you are agnostics. You're not sure you believe in words, and maybe not in God, the so-called maker of words. So you find this whole endeavor suspect. Of course, and bless you. The world—and Christian culture—provides way too many reasons to be skeptical. But I'm going to ask for a little "willing suspension of disbelief," as Samuel Coleridge advised,[1] which is to say, I'm asking you to ditch your doubt for just a few chapters and give it a whirl. I'm not here to prescribe content; I'm here to walk beside you, to equip you to write your stories, whatever they are, whether they're full of faith, doubt, anger, or disbelief.

If you are reading this book alone, I hope these pages will feel like your own personal classroom. Writing can be exhilarating and yet also lonely at times. We're more than enough, you and I and the others whose stories and experiences I have included in these pages. You can indeed work through this book and write stunning stories on your own. But I have to tell you, even more is possible. Over the decades, I've been astonished at what happens when people gather to write and tell their stories together. Writing in community, with a tangible, empathetic audience, often sparks stories that are rich in details, emotions, and insights. More than this, I've seen lifelong friendships form around this shared endeavor. Before you begin, as you think about whether to move through this book solo, with a few friends, or with a class, glance ahead to chapter 4: Your Stories Together. It will give you a glimpse of how to gather people together and what can happen when people share their voices and their work.

No matter how or why you've come to this book, or what stories you're hoping to unearth, or whether you come to these pages alone or in a class, we're going to learn together how to discover and communicate the truth of our lives with beauty and clarity. In some ways, it will be simple. I'll lay it out straight and easy, no matter if you're a first-time writer or you're fifty years in. At the end of every chapter, I'll walk you through writing prompts and assignments, with practical steps for discovering and writing your story. We'll also be joined by writers like you, mostly from my classes, bravely sharing their life stories to inspire our own.

But in other ways, this journey won't be simple. Because the reality that opens up before us, in the midst of the details and memories of our lives, is always full of mystery and wonder. So I must warn you: This work is utterly addictive. Once you start, such clarity, discovery, and consolations will come to you that you will not want to stop. You'll realize that pursuing your story is also a pursuit of meaning in this wearisome life. Which means it's also a search for magic, for divine surprise, perhaps even a glimpse of God.

Why does this practice of unearthing the truth of our stories matter so much? Why am I spending so much of my life investing in others' words? I've seen what happens when we bury our past, when we refuse to look behind, at either the tragedies or the joys or any of the million little moments that make up our lives. I've seen in my own family all that's lost—to all of us. And I've seen what happens when we dare to overcome the silence. The morning I am writing this, I got an unexpected email. It was from Carrie, a quiet, unassuming woman who came to a workshop four years ago and insisted she could not write; she had nothing to tell. She sent a story, the first I'd read from her. It was about her brother, his near-fatal plunge over a waterfall, how her mother abandoned her and her siblings when she was thirteen and she had to become the mother. How later she joined her brother on his long-distance trucking routes before his dementia set in, damage from the fall. How she came to understand and reconcile with her mother decades later. Her story was so full of pain, love, and breathtaking details, it made me cry. Carrie wrote, "I think I have many more stories I must tell."

Your story matters. Let me help you find and tell the truth of your story. A compelling story. A crafted story. A healing story. A bigger story. And in the finding and telling of this story, I promise you'll live it too.

CHAPTER ONE

YOUR BIGGER STORY

Witnessing

In this one book are the two most interesting personalities in the whole world—God and yourself. The Bible is the story of God and man, a love story in which you and I must write our own ending, our unfinished autobiography of the creature and the Creator.

**FULTON OURSLER,
IN *THE WONDERFUL WORLD OF BOOKS***

WHEN I ENTERED ninth grade, my sister and I were bused from our village school to Belmont High, a regional high school two towns away. This was the year I leapt the fence. I was tired of being the "good girl," virtually the only one in my class who paid attention, who sympathized with the teachers, who tried to help hold chaos at bay. The first-through-eighth-grade elementary school we attended in this New Hampshire village was a war zone, where second graders threw ice balls at the teachers and hit them. Where my classmates ridiculed the teachers to their faces. Where the fifteen- and sixteen-year-old eighth graders cornered me and my siblings, threatening to beat us up every week. But I was in high school now. A new school. Another town. People were civil here. Maybe I could have friends. I sidled up to the popular kids. Occasionally I went to their houses on the weekends, where we'd sneak drinks from the liquor cabinet, smoke cigarettes, and saunter down the street at midnight. I was fourteen and weary of being an outsider my whole life. But I never made a good bad kid. I loved school too much. Especially my English class.

Mrs. Butler was my ninth-grade English teacher. I see her now, in her gray cardigan buttoned at the top with a single button, a single strand of pearls around her neck, her sensible pencil skirts, her oxford blouses, her sturdy shoes, her brown hair in a kind of bouffant that ended up swirled in a bun behind her head. (Surely there was a secret sartorial manual circulating among women teachers at the time—and it was never updated past the late fifties). It was the early seventies then, and boys and girls alike were slouching about with a world-weary irreverence, wearing cropped tops and flared hip-huggers quilted with patches, their long hair parted in the middle. Mrs. Butler, on the other hand, wore a general bewilderment about the age and the wildly dressed students she found herself among.

I felt sorry for her, even as I showed up in my own kooky clothes: a gray rabbit-fur, ankle-length coat I found in our attic, which I paired with purple hot pants and platform shoes. Or a pair of old floral pants my sister had sewn that I painstakingly turned into hip-huggers. I had no money at all, but I had a bone of daring, a scavenger's habits, and a flair for the theatrical. All my efforts pitched to hiding our poverty.

Despite Mrs. Butler's disapproval of our wardrobes and our mien, she was unflagging in her efforts to teach us English. She taught grammar, mechanics, writing style—all the usuals— but underneath her formality, she cared deeply about literature and creativity and did everything to foster interest in both with creative-writing projects. I remember one story I wrote: about a girl who lived down a snaking dirt road in an unheated house. Every morning she rose in her below-freezing room, her breath a fog, to curate her small collection of garments, to apply makeup secretively in a hand mirror. An hour later, she emerged at the bus stop a mile away, transformed.

I thought my story was a clever fabrication. I had no clue, even as I read it aloud to my class, that it was a story about me.

* * *

I have always known the facts of my life, but what it meant and how it mattered—I couldn't tell you. I'm guessing that you're the same. Of course, you know the sequence of your life, who your parents are, where you grew up, where you went to school, all that's happened since. But I'm quite sure you still don't know "the story" of your life. I'm talking about more than events. I'm talking about the meaning, the wonder, the arc of your life. Where you've been beyond all the *places* you've been. I'm talking about *who* you really are. What your true name is. Where you're going. What you have to pass on to those around and behind you.

I'm starting this book here, with you, with why *you* need to find and tell your story, because you may be the biggest obstacle here. (Am I right?) I'm guessing this because this has been true in my own life. I've always believed in the power of Story, but for years, I resisted writing my own. I spent years in undergraduate and graduate programs focused on writing and narrative, on *other* people's stories. But I began to feel restless. I was living a strange, divided life that begged to be named, explored, written. During the summers, I lived in the wilderness with my husband, working as a commercial fisherwoman on a stormy ocean off the Alaskan coast. Winters, my husband and I traveled, and I taught; we were in graduate school. I *needed* to bring language and clarity to this bifurcated life, but I was scared. My life was dangerous and risky in so many ways. As a commercial fisherwoman in Alaska. As a married woman who knew little about how to be married. As a daughter from an unraveling family. There were mines by land and by sea. How could I write about any of this?

Almost ten years after college, I enrolled in one more graduate program to figure it out. Saying, "I want to learn how to write a nonfiction book" felt like saying, "I want to learn how to swim on the moon." But I did it. Wrote the book. (And don't you love language, the way I just compressed two years of agonizing work into a three-word sentence that makes me sound like some kind of genie who blinked and nodded this book into existence?) Oh the labor of it! The insecurities! The uncountable drafts!

But it was safe! I wrote about Alaskan women in commercial fishing. I told the stories of forty others, women who were tougher, more authentic, more worthy of attention than me. When a university press called to accept the manuscript I had sent on a fluke, I was stunned. I was sure it was a mistake. I didn't know any writers. No one in my family was in the professions or the arts. We were ordinary, invisible people. If there was a cardinal sin in my house growing up, it was pride. Calling attention to yourself. Thinking that you were special in any way. (*You're going to publish my book?*)

I was thirty-eight when it released, and underwater with babies, toddlers, and teaching. But I had hope now. And I couldn't stop writing. I began another book, this one a sure hit with the New York publishing crowd: a collection of essays about hunting, carrying water, digging an outhouse pit, washing fish-fouled jeans in a semicomatose wringer washer. In short, my life in the Alaskan wilderness, none of it the purview of well-showered and high-heeled urbanites. But improbably, *Awake on the Island of Listen* landed me a hot New York agent. (The heat cooled, though, when I had to make an appointment six weeks in advance to snag a fifteen-minute call with her. I was clearly on the bottom of the dogpile).

But Kate[1] did me an enormous service. Here's how our first official phone call went:

"Leslie, I really like these essays, but there's one problem: You're not in them."

"I know," I replied. "That's the point. The book is the story of a place. About topics much bigger than me: about the ethical dilemmas of killing animals, about water, so many other things. It's about universals."

"Yes, but we don't care about universals unless we care about you. You're completely absent from this work. No one's buying essay collections. You're going to have to turn this into a memoir. This needs to be about you."

"A memoir?" And in the next few seconds, I silently listed every objection to writing about my life that you may be listing right now. Let's see how closely our lists align:

- My life is not that interesting. What do I have to write about?
- I am unworthy to tell my stories. I'm a nobody. No one will care.
- I'm scared to look behind me, into my past. There are mistakes and failures that I can't face. I just want to move forward.
- I'm not a real writer. I have no idea how to write a memoir.
- I can't write the truth. I'd like to stay married. I'd like to stay in my family.
- My life story? Aren't there enough memoirs and life stories out there already? Who needs another one?

Kate was much too busy to hear all these complaints, so I kept my answer short.

"Uhhhhh, no, Kate. I can't do that." And I hung up.

Memoir was a dirty word. I equated it with first-person, tell-all stories by strippers in smoky bars, and tabloids featuring disgraced politicians and ravaged movie stars flinging fresh scandals at every shopper in the checkout line. I couldn't do it. I would continue to write impersonal essays detailing the complexities of the natural world, with no cost to myself. *And,* for extra measure, without revealing my Christian faith, which was suspect in most quarters and would harm my fledgling literary reputation, if I possessed such a thing.

But here is the beginning of my conversion. A writer came along, Frederick Buechner, who spoke such sense and truth that I began to reconsider my antipathy toward personal writing. In his book *Telling Secrets: A Memoir,* Buechner writes,

> My story is important not because it is mine, God knows, but because if I tell it anything like right, the chances are you will recognize that in many ways it is also yours. Maybe nothing is more important than that we keep track, you and I, of these stories of who we are and where we have come from and the people we have met along the way because it is precisely through these stories in all the particularity, as I have long believed and often said, that God makes himself known to each of us most powerfully and personally. If this is true, it means that to lose track of our stories is to be profoundly impoverished not only humanly but also spiritually.[2]

Buechner's memoirs recount quiet moments, moments no one else would notice, yet through his questioning eyes and pen, he captured a sacredness and a beauty in the midst of the quotidian that opened my own eyes. In *Secrets in the Dark,* he identifies a choice that is presented to us every day: "Either life is holy with meaning, or life doesn't mean a damn thing. You pay your money and you take your choice."[3] I already believed that washing clothes, fishing for salmon, hand-digging a well were all sacred in some way and worthy of exploration and record. But could it be possible that *my* story was "holy with meaning" as well?

Then I encountered the memoirist Patricia Hampl, who nudged me further. She wrote, "For we do not, after all, simply *have* experience; we are entrusted with it. We must do something— make something—with it. A story, we sense, is the only possible habitation for the burden of our witnessing."[4]

Who does not carry these burdens? Might it be possible to make a home for them? And might the burden be lighter because of it?

It took a month to get another phone appointment with Kate. The next call went like this.

"Remember you asked me to turn that essay collection into a memoir?"

"Yes, of course."

"Okay, I'll do it. "

"Good. I knew you would."

Then I got brave. "So, how do you write a memoir?"

She laughed, or something equally unhelpful. "You'll figure it out."

It wasn't easy to invite that *I* into my house. I had to learn so many things. (One of which was, don't clean the house before you let her in!) But deciding to write my own story changed my future. It changed my past. I believe it will change yours as well.

For now, remember the first time you ran away from home with your little brother, when your mother had kicked you out of the house? And how you held hands, terrified, down the winding road while cars rushed past, and you turned around when your fear of the cars finally overcame your fear of your mother?

And who else knows how you've cared for your daughter with cerebral palsy all these years, feeding her every bite of food, singing Beatles songs with her?

Remember when you took your son to the mountain outside town to watch the Christmas fireworks and he lost his shoe over the cliff and you ended up piggybacking him down the rest of the trail while you both sang "Deep and Wide"?

Do you see? It all matters. In a divine economy, none of these moments are wasted. Not the fall of a chickadee from your tree or the wandering of a rebellious sheep or the loss of a strand of your hair goes unnoticed by God.[5] And since the One Who Is Running All Things, including galaxies, takes care to notice lost sheep, dying sparrows, and falling hair, we should notice as well. Writing helps us notice what God notices. So write your story because God attends to every moment of your life, and you should too. Writing is a form of attention, a form of prayer, a form of listening to God. Even when God feels distant, through writing, through this book, we have a new way to aim our eyes, to tilt our heads to hear.

If you could see me here, you'd see me leaning in close, and maybe even whispering: *Writing the stories from our past enables us to live them again, but this time we live them wiser, better.*

*　*　*

The bus my siblings and I took to school and back every day didn't take us home. Every afternoon, those two-way doors would whoosh open and deposit us at the bottom of a hill. It was almost a mile up that steep, winding road to our house at the top. At an elevation of eight hundred feet, the hill was almost a mountain. Our legs knew it was a mountain. Every morning we ran down that mile-long mountain to catch the bus, and every day after school we waited forty-five minutes for the second run of the bus, and we were at the very end of the forty-five-minute ride. Then we slung our books against our chests, put our heads down, and pushed ourselves up that last long mile. We leaned against that mountain during rainstorms, lightning, and thunder, in zero degrees. Our gas budget—a dollar a week—wouldn't allow a daily drive up and down the mountain. And we had legs, didn't we?

Our bus driver was Mrs. Fifield, a tall, heavy woman with short, black hair. I was afraid of her. She'd yell at the rowdy kids who sauntered on board with greasy hair and crooked grins, insults and fists, ready to fight. We'd slink into our seats, hoping they'd leave us alone. But she was not to be tampered with. She kept an eye on us, glancing up at us often in her oversize overhead mirror. Her watchful gaze made me feel safe.

For the first fifteen minutes every day, we were alone in the bus. My brother Todd and I always chose to perch in the last row. Mrs. Fifield drove fast enough, even on the dirt roads, that when the bus hit the potholes, we were launched for two full seconds of flight. It was our favorite moment of the day.

One winter day, the snow came especially hard. I was in seventh grade. School was let out early for the blizzard. The heater on the bus roared as we slid and rounded Route 3B, slowed by the sideways blasts of wind, past the collapsing house, to finally end up at the bottom of the hill. We were the last ones off.

The snow fell like banners from the trees, the road was barely visible, and as the bus crunched to a stop, five of us pulled on our mittens and hats, cinched our coats tight, and readied to enter the storm. I saw Mrs. Fifield looking back at us and then looking out the windows, shaking her head—and then the unthinkable happened. The engine roared, and we lurched forward as Mrs. Fifield pulled the massive wheel to the right. She was turning up our road. Our jaws fell open. We caught one another's eyes. No one gave us rides up the hill. Ever. Now, in this blizzard, the bus was going to climb our treacherous mountain? It was madness. Maybe we wouldn't even make it. But I was filled with an inexpressible light. Mrs. Fifield was carrying us up the mountain. I didn't know anyone could be this kind. And I wonder now if Mrs. Fifield hit those potholes running just for us.

*   *   *

How strongly the past pulls, even now. But don't worry. I will not urge you to wrangle a shiny lining from the death of your sister, from your prodigal son or your lost marriage. As I talk about finding a bigger, better story, I'll be talking a lot about telling the truth. After thirty years of writing and naming, I know this: Often, redemption comes simply by bringing language—which is bringing light—to the silence. Every time we lock up a person, an event, even an entire decade in the Closet of Forgetting and Denial, we're robbing ourselves of the strength and wisdom that can come from those experiences.

Those events came to us, I believe, with some kind of meaning, maybe even purpose. If God is in and through our stories, surely he means something by the "burden of our witnessing." Just as we've been shepherded into pastures by quiet rivers and through shadowed valleys, we get to shepherd and steward these burdens, all of them—the beautiful, the brilliant, and the horrid. Through telling and writing, we have another chance to reclaim and redeem those moments. And sometimes they are redeemed simply by being faced and called out of the dark. When we can name our ghosts, they haunt us less.

Do you need one more reason to write your story? Here it is, from an astronaut who came to one of my workshops in Alaska. She had flown four missions to the space station and held the record, at the time, for the longest stay in space. She had been on the cover of *Newsweek* and the subject of dozens of articles. "I have to write my story because if I don't, someone else will," she said, with a steely gaze. "And they won't get it right."

I have so much to share about all of this. Know this for now: Your stories are bigger, more important than you know right now. Bring them out from the dark. From silence into words and voice. Notice what God notices. Answer back. Your story will only get better.

Your Turn!

I'm going to guide you through this writing process chapter by chapter, but my words are only invitations to yours. In the end, your words in response to mine are what will matter most. (I can't wait to read some of the stories that will come from these pages!) In this section, at the end of every chapter, I'll include writing prompts and assignments. Most of the chapters will include two sample life stories written mostly by people in my classes—people who are not professional writers but who, like you, are finally answering the call to pen their story.

As you write, let go of any fears about writing perfectly or even well. We're not attempting grammatical or literary perfection. We're simply remembering, writing freely and joyfully and with encouragement for one another. Here's the card to make it official:

Get Out of Grammar Jail Free

This coupon entitles the bearer to write freely and joyfully without guilt or anxiety about grammar, sentence structure, or anything else your English teachers didn't like.

REDEEMABLE EVERYWHERE.

NEVER VOID.

YOUR STORY MATTERS

As you write, spend as much time or as little time as you want on these writing prompts. Write one story or ten. Make it one page or ten. This is guilt free. Go and write, and see what happens!

1. Let's begin with a simple question: Why did you decide to read this book? What are your goals right now for reading and working through this material?

2. Many people who show up in my classes have been waiting for years to write their story. If this is you, too, what are some of the reasons you've waited? Make a list of your concerns and obstacles.

3. Because you're holding this book now, I suspect you've already answered some of these fears and concerns. Write down your responses now to those fears. If some are yet unanswerable (like "What will my father say?"), leave them blank—for now. As you go through this book, I believe you'll write past and through every one of these concerns. You *are* going to do it: Write the stories you have waited so long to write!

4. In this chapter, I recount riding the school bus. How did you get to school each day? Describe that process in writing, and any particular stories that come to mind.

5. Read the following essays, which are both about a childhood experience with God. Then write about an early encounter you had with God, or with a sense of something beyond your understanding. What happened? Write to discover—who knows what you will find!

GROWING TALL

By Arabah Joy

I was only four, but the memory is clear. Church was over. I found myself once again out back with Michelle O'Reilly. I don't remember who started the fight, but she shoved me facedown into the bush. Blades from the scratchy plant bit my bare legs. She stood over me for a moment, sunlight filtering through strands of her hair, obscuring her face. The bush tangled around me, and the fire ants found my legs before I did.

Propelled by flames, I charged after her. I soon caught her, grabbed her arm, and took revenge the only way a four-year-old knows how—I bit. Sinking my teeth right solid into her arm felt glorious . . . but the satisfaction was short-lived. Michelle screamed and ran to her father, yelling, "Arabah bit me!"

The crowd who gathered, filled with holy indignation, expected, even demanded, punishment for such a blackhearted deed. Back in the midseventies, God was foremost a God of justice . . . or at least, that's what my child heart understood.

The O'Reilly family folded their arms slow and tight across their Sunday best and leaned back against the hood of their truck. The Beck and Morrow families followed suit. Dread coursed through my body at what was coming.

My father, with tight lips, walked me to the side of the church to the oak tree, the young one with the tender branches.

"Pick your switch," he told me. This is how it always was: slow. Calculated. Bone-chilling. I wasn't yet old enough to understand which branches, in their seasoned years and weathered maturity, were allies. I picked one I could reach, young and vulnerable, like me.

For the third time that holy day, my legs stung, red welts blistering to the surface up and down my thighs and calves. When my punishment was over, I dutifully apologized to Michelle and her family, face hidden in shame, before being sent to the back seat of the car. The adults still had their conversation to finish. Justice demanded I, the sinner, sit with my guilt.

Peeking through the glass of the back-seat window, I caught the looks of the church crowd. They approved of my father's immediate and appropriate action. I watched him shake his head at his worm of a daughter.

Then Jackie came to wait with me in the car. Jackie, the man whose approval I desperately wanted, the one who groomed me to need it and then took advantage of it for years after. His eyes crinkled in mirth as he saw my legs. "Did you get a switchin'?" He laughed at me.

It wasn't funny to me. Back then life wasn't funny, and God wasn't either. I'm not sure how one can grow smaller, but in the back seat of the car with Jackie that day, it's what I started doing. That's the way I grew all during childhood: small.

But something changed one day a few years later. Every day I would ride the bus to the Christian school to be taught what good Christians should know and do. I learned how to act. I learned how to do good, all the while knowing deep down I'd never *be* good. I was too deeply stained for that. The gospel simply wasn't for me.

This day we were traveling down Sydney Washer Road, that long strip of gravel that took us from our rural town into the big city. Mrs. Myers had the lights on in the bus, which meant we all had to be silent because she was having a bad day. We passed Janice's house with the big, green pond out front. I knew the Owenses' trailer park was coming up soon. That's where Michael lived with his alcoholic father. One. Two. Three. I tried to count the trees along the embankment as the bus sped down the road. Counting was a great distraction, and soon I was breathing easy again.

Everyone was silent. Perhaps the silence that morning provided the margin for me to hear, for somewhere around that run-down trailer park is where I heard the still, small voice.

"Heidi." He spoke directly to my heart, calling me by my given name. "I love you."

I wondered at the words I'd just heard. I'd never heard them before. I didn't hear them again. That was it. It wasn't an exegesis of the gospel or a four-point message delivered by a pastor. It was four simple words spoken straight to my shattered, hopeless heart.

With those four words came enlightenment. Understanding. No, I still don't understand how children are abused and no one seems to care. I don't understand how mothers and fathers can despise their own blood, or how pastors can be self-seeking and Christians can be so hypocritical and this world can be such a horrific place. There are many things I don't understand.

But this is what I did understand that day: I understood that the heart of God is good. I understood that my life mattered to him. I understood that I was seen and known by a God I thought I'd never be good enough for.

On that dusty back road in the middle of nowhere, to no one else and without the slightest fanfare, the God of the Universe whispered that the gospel was for me. Yes, even for me.

INNOCENCE

By Ann Conway

I do not remember the precise moment that I felt God as a child because I cannot recall him not being present. Very early on, I felt God was incarnated everywhere, that he was waiting to be seen.

This was not because my family was devoutly Catholic, and our lives infused with religion, but because of a primal sense of grace, embodied in the presence of my aunt Gabe, my mother's unmarried sister. She lived with my parents, two brothers, and me in a small, gray house in the Mount Pleasant neighborhood of Providence, Rhode Island. My mother had gone back to work as a teacher when I was four, so I was cared for largely by Gabe, who worked a split shift at a nearby hospital cafeteria and thus was free during the hours between breakfast and "dinner," as we called lunch, and before supper.

Gabe was in her forties when I was born. She was perhaps an unlikely candidate to be God's emissary—handsome, wisecracking, full-bodied, and pretty much toothless. My aunt had dropped out of ninth grade and, by the time I came along, had worked for twenty years in a hospital cafeteria.

"I had my fun, kid," she said of her youth in Prohibition-era Providence. After a day on her feet, in the evenings Gabe often drank Narragansett beer and smoked unfiltered Pall Malls. She loved delicacies like liverwurst and pigs' feet. But she always went to Mass, never swore, and never wore pants.

Gabe had a lot of the child in her and was without pretense. "I'm the dumb one!" she'd crow, speaking of her more educated brothers and sisters. She was never ashamed of who she was or what she did, which to me meant that God was close by. Security in the self can bespeak deep faith.

The outings I took with Gabe as a small child reinforced my sense of grace. I seemed to smell God everywhere, especially via the luscious scent of moist earth and ripening tomatoes in the hospital greenhouse. I felt God in the small rippling brook in the middle of Pleasant Valley Parkway, where my aunt and I floated twig boats during her breaks. I heard God in the ticking grandfather clock that graced the large, empty dining room where I sat and colored while my aunt, who was the cashier, sat at the head of the adjacent cafeteria line. I felt God when I sat with my aunt after work in her tiny bedroom off the parlor, where she polished her shoes with white liquid polish and let me make dolls out of all her Kleenex. It was peaceful and safe, and I felt I was under the shelter of God's mighty wing.

On her days off, we strolled down Chalkstone Avenue, the main shopping district of Mount Pleasant. What may have seemed mundane to an adult was to me emblematic of the world's splendors. I felt that sumptuousness when we visited Walcott's 5 & 10, with its numberless shelves of cheap toys, cosmetics—including the rouge, powder, and crimson lipstick my aunt favored—and all kinds of school supplies and stationery.

I felt God when we visited the cobbler, a bent, old Italian man who sat at his bench in a tiny storefront on the corner of Chalkstone and Academy avenues, and in the Superior Bakery with its enormous glass cases full of row upon row of jewel-like pastries—amaretti, sfogliatelle, tiramisus.

Like many in the neighborhood, Gabe loved to tell stories. When I learned to read, I was amazed, thinking that through these new stories, I could go anywhere: back in time, forward, to all countries. I believed that the startling miracle of reading came from God.

Throughout her life, my aunt took on special requests from God, such as loving people who were difficult or lonely. She was always running errands for somebody. In my early life, she shopped for Kate Mohan, an ancient, miserly spinster whose family had owned the The Beehive, a barroom down the street.

I remember Kate, impossibly old, hunched in a kitchen chair near her manic parakeet, Jippy. As she dictated a grocery list for Gabe's trip to the A&P, I wandered through the tenement. The parlor was stuffed with marble-topped tables and old-fashioned lamps with crystal prisms, like in the movie *Pollyanna* with Hayley Mills, which Gabe and I had adored.

When Kate died, she left two hundred dollars to Gabe and sixty thousand to the Society of St. Vincent de Paul, which made my aunt roll her eyes and mutter darkly.

She got over it. I have never met anyone so unattached to possessions, to money. Nevertheless, she bought most of my clothes and toys. I recall her standing for hours in front of an enormous doll display at a local Christmas bazaar; she was determined to win the raffle so I could have a doll.

Maybe I had such a vivid sense of God because he was silhouetted against the dark. The years ahead would be difficult for me and for Gabe. In this account of my early years in Providence, I do not mention my parents because I retain no early memories of them at all, although I know I was petrified of my father.

As much as possible, I tried to stay with Gabe, away from both of my parents. They were a bad match from the beginning, and I never saw an iota of affection between them. When my mother returned to teaching in 1958, the marriage had broken down completely. In those days, a wife who worked outside the home was a sign of a husband's failure. My father had not gone to college and never made enough money. He told my mother that he would "break" her.

Not surprisingly, my two brothers exhibited serious behavior problems. Eventually they were diagnosed as paranoid schizophrenic and were in and out of the state mental hospital.

My parents moved us to the suburbs just after I turned nine, without Gabe. From my preteen years onward, I'd be trapped with my warring parents and disturbed brothers in a 1,100-square-foot ranch house. Gabe did the best she could to continue to provide a refuge, but the next nine years were very difficult.

However, that story is no longer my life's central narrative. I wrote this essay because I know why I am alive—because of Gabe and God. Though I have long since returned to my religion, for many years, I turned my back on God. It took a long time to get over feeling buried by all that had happened to me since I was a shy, cossetted little girl nurtured and cared for by a "nobody," an ordinary aging woman who spent her days on a high stool, handing people change from an old-fashioned cash register.

When I accompanied my aunt on our simple excursions, Gabe always remarked, "Isn't this lovely?" as if to underscore the experience. I thought that her love, which was God's love, was lovely.

When I held tightly on to my aunt's hand, I knew that God was a miracle of opulence, although I also understood scarcity—of love, of money, of parents who *were* parents. But sparseness caused love and goodness to stand out more clearly against the darkness in the world. I knew that goodness and spiritual largesse should never be taken for granted, ever. In my mind, every instance of them was cause for rejoicing.

When I was very small, I sometimes looked in the mirror and thought, *Me!* I was thrilled to be alive.

Looking back, I do not think this was narcissism; it was innocence. I was amazed that that God had created me and every other unique person; indeed, he had created everything else in the universe throughout time. Evil was real, but how beauty and virtue flourished, how they shimmered and vanquished the dark. It astounds me still.

CHAPTER TWO

YOUR FULLER STORY

Mapping

*I am inclined to believe that God's chief purpose in giving us memory is to
enable us to go back in time so that if we didn't play those roles right the first
time round, we can still have another go at it now. We cannot undo our old
mistakes or their consequences any more than we can erase old wounds that
we have both suffered and inflicted, but through the power that memory gives
us of thinking, feeling, imagining our way back through time we can at long
last finally finish with the past in the sense of removing its power to hurt us
and other people and to stunt our growth as human beings.*

FREDERICK BUECHNER, *TELLING SECRETS*

*Lord, all that I have discovered about you
I have done so by remembering.*

AUGUSTINE

IT'S THE BEGINNING of the annual writers' workshop in Alaska.
Twenty-two people sit in a giant circle in my living room. We're
eating sandwiches and fruit, our lunches balanced on our laps.
I am seriously happy. In two hours, we'll all board bush planes
and fly into the wilderness to write and explore for a week. I look
around at faces I don't yet know, men and women of all ages, from
twenty-one to seventy, here from all over the country.

After I welcome everyone to Kodiak and to my house, I settle
my turkey sandwich in my lap and ask, "Why are you here? Why
have you come all this way?" And we begin.

"I'm not a writer," says a youngish woman, "but my husband died a few years ago, and I need to capture some of our life together."

"I've never done creative writing before," says Stan, a fiftyish man with glasses, "but I've always wanted to. I have to tell about my son, Stanley, about all the miracles of his life. He's not supposed to have survived his tenth birthday. He's thirty now. People keep asking us to tell his story."

"This is my third time here," says Vina, a Filipino woman who has become a friend. "I'm working on a piece about my father, who was in the death march at Bataan, and melding that with my mother's Alzheimer's. I'm not sure how it's all going to work, but I'm really excited about it."

"I don't know if I'm a writer or not. I just know I love words, and I think they can teach me something," says Sara, a twenty-one-year-old woman. "I want to see where they take me."

"I want to write about adopting my daughter, and all God has done through that, but I don't know where to start," says Heather, a petite woman from Wisconsin.

I know how everyone feels right now. We're standing on a precipice, looking out over our lives.

I felt the same way as I hung up the phone with Kate, my New York publisher.

She wants the story of my life? She wants my story? Where do I begin? Do I start with my first memory—the spider on the wall over my crib? Who cares about that and the thousand other details of this sprawling, uncharted, stupendous mess of a thing called my life?

And I know most of you reading this could stand beside me in a chorus line with your own questions. *How much can we pass on? How much matters? How many turns and switchbacks, how many jobs, surgeries, how many weddings and grandbabies, science projects, camping trips, funerals? It's overwhelming. Must we really account for all of this?*

Let me stop this nervous dance with one word: No.

Covering the entire scope of a life is not possible. And this is why so many never start. No matter where I am, when someone asks me what I do for work and I say, "I'm a writer; I write books," the response is often the same: "I've got a book I've always wanted to write," or "Everyone tells me I should write a book about my life." Some of them are young and they've traveled the world or survived terrible things. Some are in their seventies and eighties. They're *still* waiting to write their story. If I am in the airport or the grocery store, keeping eyes on my watch, I smile, nod encouragingly, and let their words pass. But if I have even two minutes, then I answer back something like this:

I know you've got an amazing story. But you have to let go of one word: that four-letter word book. *Toss it out. Take down that navy-blue, hard-bound tome with the gilded title on the spine that's next to the Harvard Classics and throw it out. Don't try to write a book. Just write some stories.*

They always look puzzled at first, then in the next second, relieved, as if a whole shelf of leather-bound volumes had just been lifted from their chest. And it has.

Let me say this to you, too. Never mind "the book" right now. Never mind three hundred pages of the one story everyone says you must write. Set aside for now something I said in the last chapter, about discovering your story, as if there's only one, and somehow you must make it all cohere. Dump that load. Throw open the library doors and windows. There's a process, a way to walk into this. And right now, it's just about *remembering*. That's all you need right now. I want to send you out of the stuffy library and into the whispering fields of memory.

Remembering is a crucial activity for all of us. We will not know who we are without remembering.

The Hebrews in the Old Testament were called again and again to remember. In the book of Deuteronomy, they're about to enter the land God has promised them—a new life and land where milk and honey flowed from every ravine! So much anticipation!—*but* even after wandering and longing and salivating for their new home for forty years, they aren't yet ready to cross the threshold. They can't cross over without these words:

> However, be careful, and watch yourselves closely so that you don't forget the things which you have seen with your own eyes. Don't let them fade from your memory as long as you live. Teach them to your children and grandchildren.
> DEUTERONOMY 4:9, GW

What are they remembering? "But you shall *remember* that you were a slave in Egypt and the LORD your God redeemed you from there."[1] And in many places, God tells them specifically what they're to remember about their story: "Tell in the hearing of your son and your son's son the mighty things I have done in Egypt . . . that you may know that I am the LORD."[2]

They're to remember who they are, where they've come from, and how they've gotten there. And this story is completely wrapped around God's story: who he is and all he's done with them, for them. Without this remembrance, they are lost.

And so they were. They did forget who God is, the miraculous ways he freed them to make them his people, his daughters and sons: "And the people of Israel did not remember the LORD their God, who had rescued them from the hand of all their enemies on every side."[3] In fact, the whole history of God's people in the Old Testament is the story of the rise and fall of kings who do evil because they forget God. Then occasionally a righteous man emerges who "remembered" God.

Listen. I know I'm going all preachy here, but this is monumental for all of us, no matter what we believe about the Bible: The past is not done. It lives on in us, no matter how cleverly we disguise ourselves, no matter how fast we try to run from it. When we don't turn and look behind, we lose our way. Even our very selves. Dan Allender writes,

> Rather than living a life of freedom and creativity that finds meaning even in the meaningless places in our past, we purpose to forget. . . .
>
> Forgetting is a wager we all make on a daily basis, and it exacts a terrible price. The price of forgetting is a life of repetition, an insincere way of relating, a loss of self.[4]

Which stories should we remember and pursue? Only you can answer that. For me, I knew the memoir I was writing for Kate would not be the story of my life. The whole of my life was too overwhelming and I sensed, even as I began, that no reader would follow me through those brambled trails. I knew this work would focus on my move to Alaska and the new life I was still struggling to define and live. That window would be enough.

The first summer I began work on the memoir, I scratched out a time line in pencil on yellow legal pads. Into that single horizontal line, I staked a peg, labeled it with an approximate date. I remembered my first visit to Alaska and to this island off Kodiak Island. How at nineteen, it was my first time in a plane, how I landed in a tiny village in a floatplane and was met on the beach by the family I'd soon belong to. I remember the sweater I was wearing: bright yellow, red, and green, flashy and optimistic. I remember the first time in a skiff the next day. Then the first time fishing in the skiff. The first time seeing the island I thought I would live on for every summer the rest of my life. I remembered working with my husband to build the house that winter, that whole year just the two of us on an island with no contact with the outside world.

I marked another stake years later, unexpectedly moving to another island. The birth of our daughter. The Exxon oil spill. Cleaning the beaches with shovels and rakes.

One memory triggered another. The time line marched across pages, and I laid them out on the table, one after another. Railroad tracks, horizontal and vertical marks across the expanse of my days. I took my time. I didn't rush.

And already it began, a sense of relief. My childhood and even my early years in fishing were all cast in a cloak of secrets. As I marked down my memories and turning points, some fleeting and fragmentary, others vivid and overwhelming, I felt lighter. It was freeing to bring words and language to some of those memories. And I hadn't even begun to write yet.

I didn't yet know the science of "remembering." Scholars and social scientists have studied the cost of keeping secrets. Protecting secrets saps our strength, erodes our health. When we suppress and hide events in our lives, we have no means of integrating them into our experience. We think keeping secrets is good, that it keeps us from obsessing or being stuck on whatever that hard truth or event is. But of course, the opposite happens. What we try to hide will show up everywhere.[5]

When we intentionally map out the pieces of our lives, the strangest and yet most ordinary thing happens. We are mapping *chronos* time, the Greek word for time that measures the earth's journey around the sun, the steady ticktock calendar of our days and years—and then some pencil marks will drop us through the floor into *kairos* time. *Kairos* is the other word Greeks use for time, and it is time beyond measuring, beyond quantifying. This is the now from another *now*, and there we are, my newborn daughter and I both lying on the sawdusty, plywood floor of the new house, gazing at each other. She is fussing and squirming, just four weeks old and frustrated she cannot go where she wants, and I am exhausted from her colic, no longer seeing out through the windows of our half-built house the whales that spout outside in the bay. I lie beside her in a red corduroy shirt, seeing only her wide brown eyes, her appetite for always more. And I don't know if I'm going to survive this love, these nights and days on this wilderness island that blur into the unending fatigue of the sleepless *now*, a love that surely will kill me—yet I am dying happy every day because I gladly give my body to this being who is teaching me how death and love are so much the same. This is just a moment, just three minutes. Does this belong on my time line? I mark it.

And the piercing of that tent peg moves to another, earlier moment, and I go again, falling or rising into one of the scariest moments of my life. It is blowing forty miles per hour, the sea a whirlwind of white. I have been given the job of running the skiff, alone, a mile down the channel, into the breaking waves to catch the net in the water and somehow to hold on, to hold on against the wind and sea and to tie on and wait, and I am pregnant and don't know to say no to this impossible task. I mark it on the railroad tracks even though I am afraid to think about it or write about it. But I can worry later, whether to write about it or not. For now, I stake it down because it happened. And that's enough for now.

As you enter the fullness of your own story, begin with the big events marked on your chronos time line. Within those, you'll find kairos events that beckon you deeper. Right now, there is no hierarchy of importance. Mark whatever comes.

Another way to begin is to ask yourself, *What have I been entrusted with? What "burdens of witnessing" have been "entrusted" to me?*[6] Put those down. Map them on your time line. Or make a list. Here is part of my list, burdens of witnessing that come to me in no particular order:

- growing up rebuilding old houses
- a woman in commercial fishing
- living in Alaskan wilderness, fighting isolation
- two unplanned pregnancies in my forties
- raising six kids
- forgiving my father

These "witnesses" might lead me in another direction. I might feel more comfortable drawing, choosing an image as a metaphor for part of my life's journey. When I think of the decades of raising my children, I think of a tall tree with deep roots. Each child is a branch. I brainstorm, adding smaller branches, hanging key events on leaves, until a redwood fills the page, rich and heavy with memories.

And don't forget to mark down stories that make you laugh! Not that make your kids or your family or your friends laugh—but that make *you* laugh. For a few years, my boys loved to tell the story of when I hit the deer in Texas at night going sixty miles per hour. Their favorite part was when I screamed just before the impact. At this point, they gave a high, girlish scream of terror and laughed uproariously. I usually rolled my eyes in quiet protest. I gave up defending myself, that I saw the mule deer in the dark but too late to brake, so I knew I could do nothing but hit it. I gave up citing the statistics of how many people are killed every year by hooves-on-the-highways. And yes, I was driving a camper, but it was low to the ground and that mule deer could have come straight through the windshield. But I was one mother before five sons. The numbers were against me, so I sat there smiling what I hoped was a saintly smile, *or* I retaliated with my own stories. *Remember, boys, how three of you begged me to lock you in the carpeted trunk of*

*our rental car for the hour-long drive into Chicago? Remember how
mad you were at me when I said no?*

I give you permission to leave out all the stories your kids tell
on you and any other story you want. And if you're still a reluctant
life-story writer, or even life-story mapper, hear this: *You* get to
decide what stories you tell. (Yes, tell the truth, but *you* still get to
choose what you tell!)

Don't forget the bus laboring up the hill in the blizzard, the
burnt turkey on Thanksgiving, the last radiation treatment and
how you took everyone out for tacos after. Start your own catalog
of witness, or follow the one written by a brilliant author nearly
2,600 years ago, a poetic pendulum that captures the swing and
range of every life:

> There is a time for everything,
>> and a season for every activity under the heavens:
>
>> a time to be born and a time to die,
>> a time to plant and a time to uproot,
>> a time to kill and a time to heal,
>> a time to tear down and a time to build,
>> a time to weep and a time to laugh,
>> a time to mourn and a time to dance,
>> a time to scatter stones and a time to gather them,
>> a time to embrace and a time to refrain from embracing,
>> a time to search and a time to give up,
>> a time to keep and a time to throw away,
>> a time to tear and a time to mend,
>> a time to be silent and a time to speak,
>> a time to love and a time to hate,
>> a time for war and a time for peace.

ECCLESIASTES 3:1-8

Maybe you want to write something that is beautiful and redeeming and that gives others hope. No matter who we are—agnostic, atheist, done-with-church, or lifelong Sunday-school teacher—we all share a human desire for the good, the beautiful. We're all, at heart, I believe, "recyclers" who want to find beauty, even in ugliness and pain. We all long for some kind of redemption.

Or maybe you know already that you want to write something "for the glory of God." What does that mean, exactly? It means, I believe, putting the attributes of God—his holiness, splendor, power, majesty—on display through our lives wherever we are. If you're a glory person like me, then don't think you must write some kind of super-Christian "testimony" with hand-painted flowers and a glistening rainbow at the end.

No matter what our impulse for writing, no matter what beauty or redemption or glory we're seeking to unearth, the "teacher" who wrote Ecclesiastes shows us that we don't have to paper over the other side of life.[7] In fact, for Bible readers, the rest of the Bible points us shockingly in a different direction. Because don't those pages deliver full doses of both sides of the catalog of witnessing? Yes, there is sowing, mending, laughing, building, dancing. But also there is uprooting, killing, weeping, scattering, hating. If I had anything to do with the composition of this holy book, I would have been a much tougher editor. I would have cleaned up the endings of some of those books, as well as the accounts of some of its heroes. Including Solomon!

Many scholars believe King Solomon himself authored the brilliant words of Ecclesiastes, yet Solomon's own life did not end well. His biographer unflinchingly summarized his last days:

> Solomon married seven hundred princesses and also had
> three hundred concubines. They made him turn away
> from God, and by the time he was old they had led him

into the worship of foreign gods. He was not faithful to
the LORD his God, as his father David had been.

1 KINGS 11:3-4, GNT

Solomon had lived a long, fruitful, extraordinary life. Couldn't
that last part just be edited out? And what about others we find
in the Bible? Samson, Jonah, and so many others whose stories
end badly. Samson is captured and blinded and dies with a last
prayer on his lips—asking God not for forgiveness but for revenge
against his enemies. Jonah, holy man of God who spent most of
his time running away from God, ends with a pouty face as God
saves Nineveh. This unapologetic truth-telling, this whole-story-
recounting continues, right on into the New Testament where
Ananias and Sapphira drop dead for their lies, and Stephen is
stoned for his faith, and on it goes.[8]

In this book of the history of God's people and in our history
now, the great forces of life swing us from tearing to mending,
from gathering to scattering, from embracing to refraining, from
keeping to throwing away. This is the reality of life for every one
of us. While we lament the heavier side of our life stories, we also
know that without experiencing pain, we cannot experience joy.
Without scattering stones, we cannot gather them. The length
and breadth of our lives will never line up straight and steady.
In our story, too, the words we braid and toss will coil and snarl
between opposites, may tangle and resolve only to knot up again.
Our story may be longer than we know now. It's a complicated
story. It's a messy story. Let it be messy, especially now. Open the
doors. Remember anything you can.

Don't write just yet—unless you have to. First, we must survey.
We map the scope and terrain. We look at the long coil of our lives,
no matter how long or short we've lived. Whether you're seventeen
or forty-three or seventy-eight, you have a lifetime of experiences.

We're not writing a book just now. We're not looking for answers just now. We're after distance and breadth. We're after wonder. We're allowing the tension of contradictions. We're seeking context. We're learning about time and timelessness. We're going to let ourselves pass through the face of the clock. We can't know who we are now without remembering.

Time is short: Map your whole story, all that you can. Let it be complicated. Don't be afraid. Find your fuller story.

Your Turn!

We've covered some important ground in this chapter, touching on a multitude of ways to trigger memories and to map out the scope of our lives. Choose the one that feels the most helpful, or try your hand at a couple of these. Spend as much time as you're able. The more time you invest, the more you'll recall and the more content you'll have to write from in the next chapters.

1. **Time line:** Make a time line for every five to ten years of your life (depending on how old you are), marking important events: places you've lived, jobs you've held, major events in your family. Then, on that time line, see if you can identity some of these events as well:

   - When you saw God at work in your life
   - When you changed in a significant way
   - When you overcame a great difficulty
   - When you struggled with your faith
   - When you wanted to give up
   - When God answered your prayers in a special way
   - When your understanding of God changed and grew
   - When you forgave someone and/or when you were forgiven

- When you sensed God's calling on your life to a particular job, place, or relationship

2. **Burdens of witnessing:** Let's revisit Patricia Hampl's words: "For we do not, after all, simply *have* experience; we are entrusted with it. We must do something—make something—with it. A story, we sense, is the only possible habitation for the burden of our witnessing." Make a list of the special events and experiences, the "burdens of witnessing" that have been "entrusted" to you.

3. **Artwalk:** Choose an image to represent your life, or if you want to be more specific and more spiritually intentional, choose an image to represent your journey of faith. (Example: a tree, a church building, a labyrinth, a house, a mountain, a road map.) Draw it out on a large piece of paper, filling it in with key events, places, and people. If you haven't used them yet, consider using the same prompts and events listed under #1.

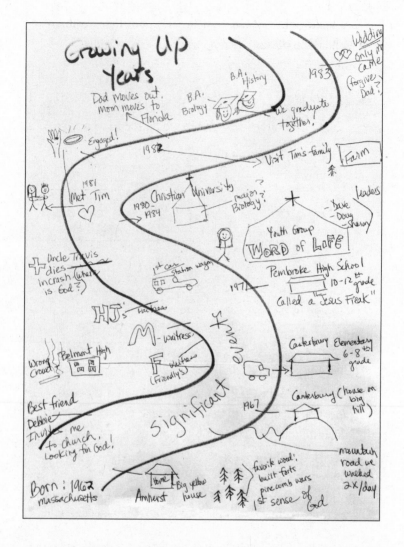

4. **The pendulum swing:** Ecclesiastes 3:1-8 gives us an extraordinary range of activities. Many of them are metaphors that may spark particular memories. Recall some times that fit under each category. (Example: Under "a time to scatter stones" I might write "my children leaving home." Under

"a time to gather stones" I might write "our first wedding—
Noah and Lizzie and how we were gathered again as a
family.")

There is a time for everything,
    and a season for every activity under the heavens:

    a time to be born and a time to die,

    _____

    a time to plant and a time to uproot,

    _____

    a time to kill and a time to heal,

    _____

    a time to tear down and a time to build,

    _____

    a time to weep and a time to laugh,

    _____

    a time to mourn and a time to dance,

    _____

    a time to scatter stones and a time to gather them,

    _____

    a time to embrace and a time to refrain from embracing,

    _____

    a time to search and a time to give up,

    _____

    a time to keep and a time to throw away,

    _____

a time to tear and a time to mend,

_____

a time to be silent and a time to speak,

_____

a time to love and a time to hate,

_____

a time for war and a time for peace.

_____

CHAPTER THREE

YOUR OUTER STORY
Scene-Making

*Long patience and application saturated with our heart's blood—
you will either write or you will not—and the only way to
find out whether you will or not is to try.*

JIM TULLY, *WRITER'S DIGEST*

I HOPE THAT after the last chapter, you've made a mess. A proper mess with charts and photos and time lines running everywhere. Maybe even a few (friendly?) ghosts have come to call. For all you neatniks out there, I'm even hoping you're a bit twitchy with all this chaos and mess. If so, you're probably like my husband, who nearly every morning noisily rearranges and organizes the pans in the cupboard because somebody has not stacked them correctly. (That would be me, cleaning up the night before, who threw the pans in any old whichway, as long as the door stays shut. Or at least mostly shut. An inch ajar is fine.) I hear him clanging and banging in the kitchen and I feel sorry for him, possessed with such need for order. But he feels sorry for me, too, though he strangely never quite blames me for the mess. I think I've convinced him that there's a fairy of entropy who comes out to play every night.

We have to make friends with that fairy, who I think probably lives in your house too. We all have a natural need for some kind of order. This is what motivates many of us to write in the first place—to clean up some of the detritus, to wrangle random events into some kind of sense and chronology. But right now, entropy and chaos are your friends. Invite them to stay for at least a little while.

We've opened a lot of doors, windows, and cupboards. Some of them may hold the usual pans and pots you keep restacking, and some, I hope, open onto an entirely new set of cutlery and pots. Where to now? How do we turn these memories and moments into stories—stories that shake and move us, stories that open the world wider to ourselves and anyone who reads them? We start with the three building blocks of storytelling: scene, summary, and reflection. And we're going to spend most of this chapter on the most neglected of the three: scene.

You already know something about scenes. Remember how in the grocery store you and your sister were having a decent, civilized discussion that may have involved a little shoving, maybe a little hair-pulling and voices at theater-worthy levels, and then your mother bombed between you, hissing under her breath, "Stop making a scene," wildly looking around for special forces with stun guns? That meaning of *scene* is definition five in the *Oxford English Dictionary*: "A public display of emotion or anger."[1] Most of us have created this kind of scene at some point in our lives—but we're after another kind.

The Writing Cooperative defines *scene* as

a section of your novel where a character or characters engage in action or dialogue. You can think of a scene as a story with a beginning, middle, and an end.[2]

In creative nonfiction, which is the genre we're writing in if we're writing directly from our lives, a scene functions basically the same as in a novel. (Fiction writers, take note!) And it functions pretty much like you and your sister hair-pulling in the aisles of Safeway: Something is happening. There's a specific setting. There's action. There's usually dialogue. The key word is *action*.

But it's not enough to have things happening. They have to happen in such a way that the reader is brought beside you. As if she's experiencing it along with you, even when it means a hair-yanking.

You know this! You've known this from childhood, when you were swept away into Willy Wonka's chocolate factory, watching with both horror and relief as Violet Beauregarde inflated into a giant blueberry, stilling those gum-chewing jaws. We all know how it feels to be ferried off into a novel, dropped from chronos time into kairos time, and there we are chasing Moby Dick with a harpoon in our hand. As a girl, I'm sure I slept in the bed next to Jane Eyre at Lowood. Isn't this the very reason we read? We read to live beyond our own single life in our own tiny cottage, to live a thousand, ten thousand lives in huts, hovels, and faraway palaces. Never forget that people are reading your life to discover and enlarge their own. They've come to live with you awhile.

That expands our definition of scene, doesn't it?

Scene takes the reader directly into the action. A scene always includes the following:

Setting: time and place of the story

A beginning, middle, and end (a mini-story)

Dialogue: people (if present) are talking

Vivid description: concrete and specific details that evoke the reader's senses

Kate reminds me of all of this on my next phone call with her, many months later. (I'm embarrassed to tell you exactly how many. Because it's a big number. It took a very long time to turn those essays into first-person stories. All those harassing voices and the fear, you know?)

"Okay, Leslie, so I got your manuscript of the memoir. I like it. You're getting it. You're getting the voice. The arc. You've definitely got movement here from beginning to end. But there's a piece missing."

"Only one piece?" I ask with relief. This is like getting an A-. I expected a B- or a C+.

"No, well, there's more."

Of course. I knew it was a C+.

"Here's the piece I want to talk about today. So—you get to Alaska, you give us some of that backstory, and then the first thing I know, we're out in the skiff and you're working those nets like a pro. You didn't start out that way, right?"

"No! Of course not!"

"Well, we need to see you when you first go out. We need to really be there with you. Take us into that boat your first time fishing. Help us feel the wind, the water. Get us wet. This is a big deal in your life and your journey, and you just skipped right over it. Take us there."

"Oh yeah, I see. Sorry I missed that. Okay, I know what to do."

And I did. She was telling me two things: that I needed backstory for context, which I would provide partly through summary. And second, that I needed scenes.

Sometimes it's hard to write about something we know well. We all have pieces of our lives that are so familiar to us, we don't even know what we know. And then we assume our readers know what we don't know we know. We skip some of the pieces they need to see, hear, taste, touch to be there with us. And our knowledge and experience are not always verbal. It may be a body knowledge. It might be a vocabulary of muscle and tendons. So it was for me. I had to stop, engage my body in the composition of those pages. How did I stand in the skiff? How did I first step into those hip-high rubber boots? How did I lean over to catch the net?

So I started. I started writing scenes of my first time actually working with my husband in the skiff. I was writing fifteen years later from that first day, but I had journals, and those early memories were sharp. I remembered the process of getting dressed, with layer upon layer of sweatshirts, hip boots, rain pants, finally layered so thick and heavy, I could hardly walk. Kind of a backwards Pygmalion story, the real person submerged under inches of fishing gear.

Then I thought of my first snack and bathroom break on the water, on an eighteen-foot open boat. There's no latrine, of course, on a boat that size. We worked all morning until it was nearly lunchtime. Duncan and his father, DeWitt, brought out the snacks from under the seat—candy bars and pop. For their bathroom break in the skiff, they asked me to turn around. For mine, I was dropped off on a rocky ledge. But it wasn't quite that simple.

But you don't care about any of that, right? I don't either. I just gave you information. I told you what you needed to know, but you weren't *with* me. I just gave you words about a time and a place far from wherever you live. So let me try again, this time as a scene:

> It's almost noon now. We've been fishing for four hours. I sit wearily on the wooden seat, looking at the fish on the floor of the skiff. There must be five hundred of them, all fat and shiny. The waves slap and slosh our skiff from side to side. I'm hungry. And I need a bathroom break, but how does this happen in an eighteen-foot boat? There is no cabin on our little wooden peapod. It's just a glorified rowboat afloat on a great Alaska sea.

DeWitt sits heavily in the bow, his black-green raincoat mirroring the dark water below. "Well, I guess I've gotta shake the dew off my lily," DeWitt intones in a gravelly voice. I can hear his Oklahoma accent, though he left forty years before, during the dust bowl. He grew up poor, picking cotton and working the land. Now he works the seas, but he moves awkwardly in the boats and never seems at home on moving water. Except now.

I smile at Duncan and DeWitt and turn around. When they're done, it's my turn.

"Let me off on that rock over there, Duncan." I point to a cove with a shelf of rock jutting out. In a moment we are there, the skiff rising and plunging in the waters swirling around the rocks. I'm nervously perched in the bow, ready to spring overboard at just the right second. My hands twitch as they grip the rail. I'm motionless but breathing hard.

"Jump!" Duncan yells as the nose of the skiff rises in the foaming surge.

"You're not close enough!" I shoot behind me. I see DeWitt sitting calmly beside Duncan as if we've done this a hundred times.

"I can't get any closer! Jump!" he shouts as the boat gurgles and sinks now in the trough.

I can't leap that distance in all this fishing gear. And if I miss? How did a simple bathroom break become a life-and-death endeavor?

* * *

Do you feel closer to the action? I hope you feel as though you're perched right there beside me in the skiff, waiting to vault overboard.

You may have noticed something else going on in this scene: summary. Scenes often include summary, a condensed form of whatever information the reader needs to make sense of the scene. We write summary with a light hand, not wanting to slow the action down. We're just sketching in the most essential information for the reader to fully inhabit the scene. This scene in the skiff includes a summary about DeWitt's background.

A question that always comes up in scene-making: What about dialogue? How can we remember exactly what people said, especially if the story happened fifty years ago? Often, we can't. (Unless it's your father-in-law, who used memorable language and the same phrases again and again.) You may not remember precisely what your sister said before she ran away, or the exact words between you and your mother when you returned to your house after the fire. We may not be able to reconstruct the exact words, but memories lodge for a reason. We often remember the tone, the sense, and the import of those words. That's all we have, any of us, unless we happened to pull out an audio recorder or a video camera during the fight, after the fire, during any of those times when the hardest, the best, and the most banal words passed between us and another. Render dialogue as closely and as fairly as you can. It will be enough.

But if your memories of a particular exchange are thin and uncertain, there's another solution: Don't use dialogue. There are many other ways to convey the scene: "I don't remember my grandmother's voice or even her words that night, but after supper, when everyone left the table, she talked to me about going to college. She believed in me more than anyone else in my family."

Writers have been rendering scene and summary for a long time. More than half of the Gospels in the Bible are scenes. Much of the Old Testament is made of scenes. How did those ancient authors (who didn't read a book on writing) know this, that we needed not some dusty account of who did what, when, where, and how, but full immersion, full attachment to those events, no matter how distant?

Consider this fantastical scene, written by Ezekiel 2,500 years ago:

> The LORD took hold of me, and I was carried away by the Spirit of the LORD to a valley filled with bones. He led me all around among the bones that covered the valley floor. They were scattered everywhere across the ground and were completely dried out. Then he asked me, "Son of man, can these bones become living people again?"
>
> "O Sovereign LORD," I replied, "you alone know the answer to that."
>
> Then he said to me, "Speak a prophetic message to these bones and say, 'Dry bones, listen to the word of the LORD! This is what the Sovereign LORD says: Look! I am going to put breath into you and make you live again! I will put flesh and muscles on you and cover you with skin. I will put breath into you, and you will come to life. Then you will know that I am the LORD.'"
>
> So I spoke this message, just as he told me. Suddenly as I spoke, there was a rattling noise all across the valley. The bones of each body came together and attached themselves as complete skeletons. Then as I watched, muscles and flesh formed over the bones. Then skin formed to cover their bodies, but they still had no breath in them.
>
> Then he said to me, "Speak a prophetic message to the winds, son of man. Speak a prophetic message and say, 'This is what the Sovereign LORD says: Come, O breath, from the four winds! Breathe into these dead bodies so they may live again.'"

So I spoke the message as he commanded me, and
breath came into their bodies. They all came to life and
stood up on their feet—a great army.

EZEKIEL 37:1-10, NLT

It's not clear whether this is a vision or in-the-flesh reality, but
one thing I know for sure: This is a scene! It's not only a marvelous example of scene (characters! dialogue! setting! action!), but I'm
going to use it another way too: as an analogy. Isn't this an image of
what we're doing when we write stories from our lives?

There we are, standing in the middle of a valley, looking out
over the bones of our past. We might be excited or despairing or
quizzical or joyous or all of these things. But how will we bring
them to life? How do we attach tendon to bone? How do we conjure up muscle and ligaments, pull fresh skin over the new flesh?
How do we resurrect the people and moments of our past? We do
it, like Ezekiel, through language. Our words can call forth and
join piece by piece by tendon by joint by muscle by skin. By which
I mean, we write scenes. And we include whatever summary is
needed to make sense of those scenes.

There's a reason scenes are so powerful and so necessary to our
stories. It might be enough to simply say we're flesh-and-blood
creatures, so we need words that awaken the past through our bodies, our senses. That sounds like reason enough. But I am greedy
and curious. Surely there is more to this need for earthy, in-the-
flesh words. If you're a God-searching person, there *is indeed* more
here. (If you're God-shy or even God-averse, feel free to skip this
part, but you'll miss something if you do.)

Who is this God who speaks to bones? He's not just a word-
speaking God, a storytelling God. Even if you believe that God's
words in his book are Holy Spirit alive, not even all this was
enough for us. We needed more. God was telling and writing

his story already through his people, the Hebrews, calling out a people for himself, but those words were not enough for them. Clearly. Because if you remember your Old Testament at all, you remember this: *Things were not going well for anyone.* (Idolatry. Rebellion. Defiance. Judgment. Drought. Famine. Fire. Enslavement. Short-term repentance, then rebellion; rinse and repeat the cycle.)

We human beings needed more. We needed more than the words of the law, perfect though they were. God knew it. He knew we needed bones and flesh and drama! So in the next story, the New Testament, God told a better, fuller story. This time his word birthed human flesh, with arteries and veins, a pumping heart, highways of nerves, with toes, fingernails, forearms, and hairy legs. The logos, the Living Word, now laughed, reclined on grassed hillsides, ate roasted fish on the beach, gulped wine at weddings, smeared dirt on a blind man's eyes, plodded through mud.

We plod through mud too. No matter how lofty our ideas or how spiritual we think we are, faith calls us to the things of this world. If our words don't conjure up the mud, the fish in the skiff, or the look in our mother's eyes, the bones of our past will lie on the floor of the valley, scattered, lifeless.

These specific details of our existence matter, and not simply as material that we dress up and animate to act out a more Christian story. We've done that already. The Christian literary tradition is lined with allegory, some of which I love. But this planet, bursting with 8.7 million species of creatures, is not just a shadow box for a future higher realm.[3] It matters now. Heaven's coming *down* to earth. So be careful not to sermonize (which I acknowledge I'm doing here!). Give us a story. Give us the earthy details. Describe the salmon's scalloped scales, the way each fish was suited in its own silver mail. How slick the mud was, like clay with tiny pebbles in it. And did you see how his mother's green eyes faded when he left and how she threw her crumpled napkin into the fireplace? The enfleshing of the words of God is not done. The Word became flesh so that now, our flesh can become word. God is writing his story through the details of our lives as well.

In a recent class, after reading this passage in Ezekiel, I asked my students to write something about bones. I asked them to "tell" a story about a time they broke a bone or experienced something related to their bones. Zandree was at the finish line of a successful battle with bone cancer. She wrote this:

> Bone marrow cancer. It was a diagnosis I expected,
> maybe even hoped for at the beginning because it meant
> the beginning of the end—no matter what that looked
> like. An end to the pain, an end to the suffering, an end
> to the depression. An end that maybe, just maybe, also
> contained a new beginning. A beginning that was going
> to mean new life, one way or the other.

That's exactly what I asked for. I gave them a few minutes to "tell" their story. When they were done, I asked them to return to that event, to those dry bones, and to "show" the story. To render it as scene. Zandree wrote this:

> The sterile-white paper gown crinkled underneath my
> breasts, stomach, and hips, as my body pressed hard
> into the cold steel of the surgical table. The drill bore
> the full weight of the doctor's heavy male body as my
> bone splintered and cracked beneath the undulating
> bit. Pain shot through my body's network of nerves like

lightning to the top of my skull and very tips of my toes in milliseconds. A single tear welled out of my right tear duct and slid slowly down the arc of my nose.

The drugs, the thought-words sludged through the mud of my mind. *They aren't working.*

I lay there, salty tears now pooling beneath my left cheek, unable to move for the power tool buried deep in my pelvis. Words exploded from the mouth of the doctor living just another Wednesday—the shot heard 'round my world.

"I can't get through her bone . . ."

Are we not there with her in those painful moments on that table? The "telling" words didn't take us there. Only the "showing" words. Listen: Scenes aren't just for your reader. They're for you, too, the writer. The one who lived through that moment, the one who survived and has now returned to tell about it, to make something of it, to send it on.

How smart do you have to be to do this? How many degrees do you need? I've had some brilliant students, people much smarter than me. People with encyclopedic minds and maybe even photographic memories. But over the decades, I've discovered that compelling storytelling isn't about intellect or education. It's about courage. It's about persistence. It's about daring to dig through vague words to get at the real, concrete world. It is through writing scenes that we discover again and again our love for this world, the goodness of this muddy material existence.

I know Kate is not thinking of any of this when she tells me I need more scenes in my memoir. I know she is not thinking of this as an exercise in metaphysics and incarnational theology. But this is precisely what it is.

As I remembered and wrote about my first day in fishing, as

I wrestled verbs and adjectives to capture the sound of the water against the wooden skiff, the feel of the salmon between my fingers, the plunge of the skiff by the rock, I remembered more. I remembered something about my father-in-law, which has since become one of my favorite recollections of him.

> We've missed lunch. We've declared a snack break, retrieving the candy bars from under the wooden seat of the skiff. DeWitt sits now, his head down, his hat askew on his head, munching his Snickers. I'm eating the same, both of us rocking in the slap of the waves against the skiff. He appears to be studying the salmon lying askew at our feet. Then he looks up at me and says, straight into my eyes, "Those are beautiful fish, aren't they?" I nod in surprise. He leans over, grunting, and picks one up with both gloved hands, holding the silver body out lengthwise in front of him. With the wonder of a boy, he shakes his head: "Beautiful fish."
>
> I look at him, trying to hide my amazement. DeWitt has seen and smelled and handled these fish for twenty years. He came to fishing in his forties and now he's in his sixties, when most people are beginning to fade. When most people begin to grow old. How is it that after twenty years of seeing and smelling and handling these creatures, he can still see them? Why hadn't they turned into faceless objects, or pieces of money? I hoped then that in twenty years, I could do the same.

* * *

As you stand in the valley, don't leave the bones on the ground, bleached, blank, silent. Speak to the bones, like Ezekiel.

Remember the wind in your ears as your family drove to your camp, how cold the river was when you fell in, the sound of your mother laughing, what your brother said, and how you burned the trout at dinner and your father ate it all before launching you, hollering, into the river one last time. Live it again. Write it. Take your readers with you into this world of glorious bodies. Tell them a real Story.

THE THREE BUILDING BLOCKS OF CREATIVE NONFICTION

Scene: A scene recreates the experience of the writer for the reader. A scene evokes our feelings, takes us directly into the action. A scene often includes

Setting: time and place of the story
A beginning, middle, and end (a mini-story)
Dialogue: people (if present) are talking
Vivid description: concrete and specific details that evoke the reader's senses

We've missed lunch. We've declared a snack break, retrieving the candy bars from under the wooden seat of the skiff. DeWitt sits now, his head down, his hat askew on his head, munching his Snickers. I'm eating the same, both of us rocking in the slap of the waves against the skiff. He appears to be studying the salmon, lying askew at our feet. Then he looks up at me and says, straight into my eyes, "Those are beautiful fish, aren't they?" I nod in surprise. He leans over, grunting, and picks one up with both gloved hands, holding the silver body out lengthwise in front of him. With the wonder of a boy, he shakes his head: "Beautiful fish."

Your Turn!

1. At the end of this chapter are two life stories that are rich in scene ("Sometimes a Fox" by Todd Johnson and "A Time to Leave" by George Linn). Before you start writing, spend some minutes with these pieces. Read them through first for pleasure. (Always the most important reason for

Summary involves *telling* the reader whatever backstory is needed to understand the scene or event. Compress the information appropriately, leaving out unnecessary details and descriptions, which can interrupt the momentum of the story.

> DeWitt has seen and smelled and handled these fish for twenty years. He came to fishing in his forties and now he's in his sixties, when most people are beginning to fade. When most people begin to grow old.

Reflection goes under the surface of scenes and summary to get at the deeper meaning, to develop the "inner story." It reveals the "story of your thought" about the events you are describing through scene:

> I look at him, trying to hide my amazement. . . . How is it that after twenty years of seeing and smelling and han-dling these creatures, he can still see them? Why hadn't they turned into faceless objects, or pieces of money? I hoped then that in twenty years, I could do the same.

reading!) Then read them through as a writer, identifying each paragraph as scene, summary, or reflection. (We'll dive more into reflection in chapter 5, but for now, label what you think seems more interior than scene or summary.)

2. Look back at the story or stories you wrote from chapter 1: an early encounter with God. Does it "tell" the story more than "show" the story? Try rewriting key moments with vivid scenes, using setting, sense-appealing details, and dialogue (if it fits). Bring your reader with you into those moments.

3. Return to your maps, time lines, your Artwalk, whatever means you used in the previous chapter to map the scope of your life. Do you feel a particular pull toward an event? Follow it, writing vivid scenes to capture that moment. Follow your passion. Follow your curiosity. Take your time and write as many scenes as you can. Help your reader see, hear, feel the setting and the events that happened, using vivid sensory details. It's okay to "overwrite." You can always trim later. As you do this, you're putting muscle on those bones. You'll soon see them walking around!

SOMETIMES A FOX

by Todd Johnson

In second grade our class at Southwest Christian Academy went on a field trip to Iroquois Park. On the drive, I imagined myself and my classmates as Iroquois Indians in fierce war paint, sporting bristled mohawks and twirling bloody tomahawks into the air. This is how boys think, so when we piled out of the maize-colored bus in a frenzy, our hands formed wah-wah pedals for our screams. We descended on the natural wildness of the park armed with our cloistered wildness—sixty shooting arrows of pent-up hyperactivity. Green trees waved welcome, beckoning us back to our primal home, but we ignored our heritage for the white man's trinkets—a playground with seesaws, swing sets, and slides.

Inside the metal play fort, a spark of danger bloomed inside me—a spirit animal was born—a wily fox, uncharacteristic and cunning. Back then, I could only describe the sensation as hunger, but not physical; no hankering in my belly for chicken or Twinkies. This hunger was spiritual—a need for new experience and freedom. It was odd because I was a child of temperance and conformity. A quiet A-student, I was not one to grasp for forbidden things or give in to impulses. So this strange fox within, with quick eyes and glistening teeth, aroused both curiosity and nervous excitement.

"Hurry up, Spencer!" Brandon yelled to the mousy boy at the top of the slide.

"I am; hold on." Spencer scanned the horizon for witnesses—potential jurors.

I stood behind Brandon, four kids back down the ladder. The fox sensed risky behavior, and it brought me to the foot of the slide. Each kid had ascended the ten rungs of the ladder, stared down the expanse of bent mercury, and then paused, as if mesmerized. Watching for teachers, they'd move their legs out over empty space, but not to the top of the slide. No. These pale savages stretched their legs around the *outer* pole—to the beam supporting the slide at a seventy-degree angle.

Like firemen, each hugged the pole with both arms and legs, then *swoosh*, they'd zip to the ground. I watched the descent, viewing them in a new light: daredevils, protesters, and shameless rule-breakers. I coveted their subversive creativity. The fox smelled blood.

"Spen-cer Gard-i-ner!" The sound of Miss Gunther's Kentucky drawl swept away all fantasies. "What are you do-eeng up thay-er?"

Spencer was midcling on the pole, ready to cherry drop.

Miss Gunther squinted up at Spencer the way I imagined Jesus eyed Zacchaeus up in his tree. Spencer, now looking as guilty as the corrupt tax collector, put his foot back on the ladder. Miss Gunther canopied her eyes with one hand and said, "You cai-n't go dow-un that wa-ay. You come dow-un the rye-ite wa-hay. No-ow!"

"Oh-kaaay," Spencer whined as the other sliders groaned in unison. In seconds, and in obedience to God's law, Spencer's butt slid down the mirrored surface.

The fox remained wary and attentive as I climbed up the slide to take my turn. I was relieved to see Miss Gunther saunter off to patrol the reservation, but I had no plan.

Then I was at the top—the pinnacle of the world. Slides feel this way when you are young, as the expanse and altitude flattens out the neighborhood. There may have been a lift in the air that decided things, dreams of tawny ancestors moving through wooded forests, or an inhalation of migratory birds heading north above *ken-tah-ten* (Kentucky), which in Iroquois may mean "land of tomorrow."[4] Whatever it was, my body sensed the oak and elm trees leaning up on their roots, rattling branches, and goading me to action. Without words, the fox within called me in seductive growls: *down the pole, down the pole, down the pole, you boy called fox.*

I paused, maybe. Hadn't Jesus been tempted by the devil— *Throw yourself down, angels will catch you.* But he wussed out. I remember my embarrassment for Jesus because he fought the devil with *words*—even worse to an eight-year-old boy, *Bible verses*! I wanted Jesus to jump, to fly like Superman. Here was my opportunity. I didn't understand it then, but maybe this was my defiant response to the devil's challenge, or maybe only a subconscious protest to my own timidity—a way to purge myself of do-gooder cowardice.

Heart thumping, I swung my legs around the pole. The fox howled. I let go—

Time and space collapsed in a fugue rush of wind, fire, and greenery. The hunger sated in an instant—my lips cottoned in the smack of freedom and the bent parabola of rebellion. The ecstasy created a pit below me. I was falling, past the outstretched arms of angels, really falling, out of control, no pole now, yellow eyes, a leaf spinning a hundred revolutions a second from the temple, earth and—snap!

blazing pain—bite of teeth on bone

My wrist took the entire brunt of the Fall—like a dry twig trod cleanly in two, my arm fractured under the heft of gravity's heel; my hand cast into fire.

* * *

Decimated. Sitting in the grass in horror, I couldn't fathom the abomination of flesh, all angles and swelling. I don't remember tears; there was intense pain. The familiar hand I had known my short life—the buttoner of shirts, the holder of toothbrushes, the wielder of pencils—obliterated by my own stupidity.

Jesus said if your hand offends you, cut it off, for it is better to lose that than to sacrifice your whole body to the fires of hell. But I didn't want to lose my hand. My hand wasn't the culprit. It was the sly fox who'd done it, the beast now conspicuously silent, cowering in some corner of my conscience.

All I could do: hold my throbbing wrist upright and pray the sinner's hopeless prayer of undoing. I called out for Miss Gunther.

When I woke in the hospital, it was hard to focus. The dots on the ceiling pulsed; I was still groggy from anesthetics. The doctors decided it was easier to put me under to reset my fractured wrist. Now conscious, I felt the weight of what I'd done in a white battering ram, a hunk of hardened plaster grafted to my arm with three portholes for bicep, thumb, and fingers.

But my parents never mentioned the incident afterwards; Miss Gunther never spoke a word of it; and I must have buried the need for absolution below my friends' swirly signatures and the itchy confines of my cast. My parents chalked up this incident to an accident—they didn't know about my fox or my sin. Maybe they should have known. My name, after all, means fox,[5] and although I do my best to keep my name at bay, he comes and goes, howling at the moon or whimpering at shadows. Sometimes, in thoughts, he may lead me back to that place where I was born—not the land of tomorrow, but a place called *Kentucky*, or as some translations put it, the "dark and bloody earth." It's there where foxes meet and where the bones of the past are broken and mended.

A TIME TO LEAVE
By George Linn

The day I left home for the Naval Training Center in Great Lakes was the first time my father didn't stand behind me. He laid no hand on my shoulder. No hand mussed my hair. I sensed no pride welling up the way it had when we'd go uptown on Saturdays and run into one of his railroad buddies hanging on to a parking meter.

"Is that the boy, Slim?" they'd ask, my father standing behind me, his hands squeezing my shoulders.

His cronies had given him a nickname obviously connected to his stature. Each time it took me by surprise. They were track men for the B&O,[6] often reeking of creosote, lifting rail and driving spikes for a living. My father, on a good day, couldn't have been more than five-feet-ten-inches tall or weighed any more than a hundred and forty pounds.

At the airport he'd turned his back, busied himself gazing up at a travel poster, only pausing long enough to run a pocket comb through his slicked-back hair. I sat at the gate alongside my mother, my twin sisters, and my three-year-old brother, who was fighting imaginary figures and making temporary landings onto my mother's lap.

"I don't know, you guys," I said.

"Too late," she said. "Go say something to your father?"

"Too late," I said. "He made it clear he doesn't want me coming back home."

"He's just afraid . . ."

"That I'll get out of here?"

"No, that you'll end up over where they're fighting."

* * *

The night before, we'd watched more news coming out of Vietnam.

Weary soldiers mired in an endless war carried their wounded by their arms and legs, their dead zipped tight in the darkness of military-issued body bags.

"If they ever wanted me again, they'd have to chase me," my father said, referring to his stint in the army. The tightened muscles in his neck became quite visible. Through clenched teeth, he said, "I wouldn't blame them all for heading to Canada."

My mother held a bowl of cream cheese and wedged a bag of corn chips between us on the couch. "Why would they want you again?" she asked. "Besides, he'll get to see the world." She shrugged her shoulders, nonchalantly dipping a corn chip into the cream cheese, quite pleased with her own commentary.

"I bet they told them that, too," he said, pointing to the television. My father's voice, usually found somewhere between non-existent and soft-spoken, became unusually strong, then cracked, as if he might break into tears. "My second week over there, they had me throwing arms and legs into the back of a truck. You tell me, how they know who's in them bags?"

It was the first time I'd heard him say anything about Korea other than that he'd slept under an ammunition truck. Then there was my mother's well-rehearsed story of how he'd sent all his money home so that they could get married. How the night he found out his parents had spent it all, he'd walked over five miles in the pouring rain to her house.

I defended myself. "I'm leaving here with a guaranteed duty station."

"You can't even swim."

"They'll teach him," my mother said, defending me.

"You just don't want me to get out of here," and before he could say it, I said it for him: "I know; if West Virginia doesn't have it, then I don't need it."

*   *   *

On the ride to the airport, my father, driving, said, "You've hurt your mother."

My mother, looking out the window, abruptly asked, "Is this the way we used to come to the Green Stamp store?"

"Uh-huh," he said, working a disc of butterscotch candy around his mouth.

My mother turned and asked, "Remember Elsie, the Borden cow? How she'd turn her head and wink at you?"

"I think so," I said.

"I wonder what happened to that sign?"

"They tore it down," my father said. "Too many fools stopping to look at it."

"I guess we were fools."

Looking back in the rearview, he said, "Your mother doesn't want you to go."

They'd gotten good at speaking for each other.

"I'll be all right," she said. "Just write me lots of letters."

* * *

"Look at him," she said, "thin as a rail, and not a hair out of place. At home I can barely pry a word out of him. Go say something to him." Her voice was nearly a whisper in my ear.

"I don't want to."

"George Jr."

I hesitated but went at her insistence. He was talking to an old man who had been wandering around the airport. As I approached, I heard him say, "He's going into the Navy."

"Anchors aweigh," the old man said, and just as quickly he was off, striking up another conversation.

"He might be a little touched," my father said.

I finally said, "I just want my freedom."

"You won't get it there."

"How come you never talk about Korea?"

"Nobody ever asked," he said, as my flight number was called.

Pushing through the turnstile and stepping onto the tarmac, I turned to see my mother. My father, barely visible, stood behind her, his hands on her shoulders. I couldn't take my eyes off my mother. She stood just inside the gate, her dark brown hair curled and slightly unkempt, wearing the torn, gray peacoat she swore was more comfortable than anything she'd ever owned. She was holding my baby brother, a twin clutching a handful of her skirt by each hip. She didn't wave but offered me a parting look I've come to believe only a mother could offer: a look telling me I was forgiven of any hurt I was about to cause or would ever cause her again.

My father and I had said good-bye, but we never touched.

* * *

The topic of Korea didn't come up again until after my mother's death in 2012 when, on a final visit, my father felt the urge to give me the Zippo lighter he'd carried during the war.

We sat on the back porch, drinking coffee. He finally opened up, telling me a story of a freezing prisoner who had asked him for a cigarette. As he told it, he rubbed his thumb over the insignia on the face of the lighter.

He said, "So I lit up a Chesterfield and handed it through the fence to him."

"That same lighter?" I asked.

He nodded.

"The next thing I knew, a South Korean soldier was beating him with a club made out of strands of barbed wire. I aimed my rifle at him and said, 'You stop that s***. We don't even treat our animals that way back in West Virginia.' Then the lieutenant stopped me. 'You let them handle their own,' he told me."

He handed me the lighter. I rubbed the Wolfhound with my thumb.

"All that man wanted was a cigarette. I knew right then, if they ever wanted me again, they'd have to chase me. I said no boy of mine was ever going to have to go through that kind of thing. And Vietnam was that kind of thing."

*   *   *

When I left home that day, during the Vietnam War, my father was only forty-four years old and was still hurting from a war that happened before I was born. I wanted his blessing; he didn't give it. He got angry instead, and before I left, he said, "You've hurt your mother, so don't come back."

I wonder now, if he had given me the lighter sooner, maybe I wouldn't have enlisted.

CHAPTER FOUR

YOUR STORIES TOGETHER

Gathering

I take seriously Flaubert's statement that we must love one another in our art as the mystics love one another in God. By honoring one another's creation we honor something that deeply connects us all, and goes beyond us.

JOYCE CAROL OATES, *PARIS REVIEW*

ALL SUMMER LONG, with Kate's words in my ears, I wrote scenes. I sat in my studio, which was a tiny shed on a dock over the ocean. When we first came to the island nine years before, this shed had been stacked to the rafters with junk that had rusted and roosted for decades: crumbling cans, old tools, jars of nails. No one had lived on this mile-long island since the 1950s. My husband and I cleaned out the shed, dragged in two sawhorses, dropped a four-by-eight sheet of plywood on top—and there it was, my desk, my office. The shed wasn't insulated or heated, so even in the summer, with the temperature in the forties, I sat in a winter coat, hunched over my legal pad or old computer, writing, remembering, with the wind whining reminders through the cracks. With six children spinning and dizzying the house up on the hill, this was my haven, silent of all but the wind, the ocean licking the pilings beneath me, the fishing boats rumbling as they passed, the crows and bald eagles screeching overhead.

I was living my own version of the starving artist, that muse-haunted writer alone in a spartan cell beside a lone sputtering candle. But I was happily aware of all I was missing: for those hours, no sink of encrusted dishes to attend to, no wailing babies, no kids' chores to manage, no tussles to referee. My studio, in all its rusty tools and starkness, was beautiful to me. For a few days, anyway.

But I was too alone, and I knew it. Who was I writing for? Yes, I was writing for myself, to make sense of my life. I was writing to find God. But who were my readers? I could not imagine an audience for this book. The only audience I had was Kate. Was I writing for Kate? Kate was my agent, but she wasn't a real reader. She was getting paid to be my reader. I knew I needed others to offer feedback and support as I wrote, but who? I felt profoundly alone as I wrote all through that summer.

I learned a lot from writing alone. But now that I've led writing groups for decades, I know what I've missed. When a community, however small, is gathered around our stories and scenes, our words come to life in surprising new ways. I'm reminded of it every time I lead a writing workshop, especially out on our island in Alaska.

It's twenty years after that first summer of wrestling words and scenes for Kate. We're in a house on the hill over my first lonely studio, on our second full day of class. I'm sitting against the wall, glancing out the window as I speak. The ocean is just a few hundred feet away. I've just asked everyone to write a scene from their time line.

"Okay everyone, we'll write for just one more minute. See if you can finish your thought." I look around the room. About half are still working their pens and keyboards. The others are glancing at me or reading what they've written, some with smiles, others with frowns. Shari is already sharing her piece with Rick, who is sitting next to her. They both stare at her page with the gaze of an archaeologist.

"Okay, good! That's our last minute."

Jim lays down his pen with a flourish. Lisa snickers at something she's written. Everyone now looks at me.

"Wow, I saw some serious smoke coming out of your pens! How did it go?"

"It was hard for me to remember details at first. I wrote about a bike accident when I was ten. But the more I thought about it, the more I remembered," Shari offers. "I just want to keep writing."

"Yeah, me too. I can't believe how writing took me back so many years. I was there with my father fixing his car," Jim says.

"Fantastic! Now, this is the fun part. Let's break up into our LifeStory Circles and share our stories. Let's do groups of four," I tell them. No one is surprised by this. The weeklong class is called a "workshop," and I've let them know beforehand that we'll be sharing our work. But the first time can be scary.

"Mine's terrible!" Suzanne groans.

"Mine's worse. I started out in one scene, then remembered a better story, so I've got two parts that don't go together," David says, sliding his chair toward the others.

"Hey, everyone, you wrote it in fifteen minutes. Are you expecting Pulitzer material here?" I say, smiling. "Of course it's rough! That's all we're doing right now—a first draft."

Chairs scrape. Pages rustle. Computers shift onto laps, and it begins. In each group of four, one person reads at a time. There's always jockeying for who reads first. And there's always the brave one, the impatient one whose story is so on fire they must read it, sharing the heat and light from the sentences that emerged from their fingers. There's always one hesitant reader, and sometimes she'll pass. But mostly, she'll read too. The others always lean in close to listen.

Today I'm not going to join a group. I just stroll around the room, looking out the windows as if I'm watching for whales, which I am doing, but I'm mostly listening.

I see Heather reading. Her hands are shaking slightly, her voice wavers. I know this is her first writing group ever. I know she's only recently begun to write. I hear some of her words. She's reading about her children, her adopted children from Russia. I hear Vina reading about her mother. In another circle, David is reading something about his father. The group by the window suddenly erupts into laughter. I look back at Heather's circle. She's wiping her eyes and others are nodding sympathetically.

I know what's happening. This is the best part of the class, when buried memories emerge. When the writer brings her own breath and voice to tiny moments and grand moments, and those moments are now heard and shared, often for the first time.

I've seen it five hundred times. How rapt the listening faces are at hearing another's words. How surprised writers are when they hear their own words aloud: David reading about his mother's diagnosis of lung cancer. Joan telling about her daughter's first day back at school after the accident. When Molly tried to sign the divorce papers and couldn't.

Last month I sat in a circle of writers from remote villages in Alaska. Darlene had never written a story from her life before, and neither had she read her words aloud to anyone. She wrote about her adult alcoholic children, how she kept trying to help them, take care of them. Her strength wore out day by day. One day, she fainted. The doctor told her she was dangerously anemic and malnourished. She could have died, he told her. She must rest and take care of herself. Darlene read her story to us slowly, her face calm but hands trembling. She ended simply with the sentence, "I, too, am important." She read this sentence with pressed lips, then looked up at the four of us with resolve. She needed to proclaim those words to us, and we needed to witness them. That truth she was finally able to speak and to share may save her life.

Yes, we write to save our own lives, to speak words into the wordless places in our lives. And many times, that is enough. But there is more. We write for ourselves, and maybe we even write for God. If so, no matter what happens to our work from there, we already have an impressive audience! But there's more: readers. The stories we write are not complete without readers. Stories, however raw and unfinished, need voice and an audience. And listening to others' stories often sparks and vivifies our own stories in response.

Heather, who continues to attend workshops, later wrote this about her first time sharing her words:

> The first time I sat in a writing circle, I felt nervous.
> My group had writers of all levels—a managing editor
> of a major magazine; several already published authors;
> and me, the most inexperienced. I had confidence in
> my academic writing ability as a Doctor of Clinical
> Psychology, but I had never ventured into the scary
> whirlpool of writing my own story.
>
> Would they rip my manuscript (and my heart) to
> shreds with criticism? Would they view my story as not
> worthy compared to their own or others'?
>
> But it turned out so differently than I expected. When
> I told my story, I felt seen and heard—two things I had
> not felt before with regards to my parenting experience.
> I could see tears well in one woman's eyes, a woman with
> her own special-needs daughter who could relate to what
> I wrote. More than all this, I could see that these women
> could relate to the universal theme of my story. We all

had experienced the pain of not being seen, of not being heard, of having our stories minimized, marginalized, not wanted.

All the writers encouraged me to keep writing, telling me my story was necessary because it could help many others. More than all the positive writing growth, I grew in my ability to share vulnerably and to receive others' stories gratefully.

Gary, a pharmacist and a new writer, was also anxious about sharing his work with others. Later, he wrote this about his experience:

Throughout the week, I found we all had insecurities in our writing skills. Rejection letters, a harsh remark from a friend, or being chided by a family member about "doing something with your life" all take their toll. I learned I was not alone. In fact, I was in pretty good company!

In my small group, we read one another's work. We listened intently as the writer would read aloud what they had written. We spoke the truth in love about how the words had an impact on us. We were writers taking a risk to bare our souls. In the end, we were rewarded for doing so because we wanted the best for one another. Our personal insecurities were held in the hands of other writers with care and acceptance.

Yes, it's a risk to open your freshly scrawled memories and even your polished stories to others. Once you do it, you'll be strengthened and encouraged; most of your anxieties will fade. But there are deeper reasons to share your work. Why are your stories so important, so powerful? Because the Book of This World is unfinished without your story. In the Bible, Creation begins with a Creator who generates the entire spinning, exploding cosmos with nothing but words: *let there be, let there be, and there was.* And God pronounced it *good, very good.* Why wasn't it perfect? It was not perfect because the world was not finished. Our work since we were given the breath of life is the same work given to Adam as the animals paraded before him: to speak back, to name all that is, to finish what was started, to offer it back to God and to one another.

Could it be that *God intended creation to be a conversation instead of a monologue?* God speaks, utters forth, and the word-birthed cosmos responds often better than we do: "The heavens declare the glory of God, and the sky above proclaims his handiwork. Day to day pours out speech, and night to night reveals knowledge. . . . Their voice goes out through all the earth, and their words to the end of the world."[1] In Jesus' triumphal entry into the city of Jerusalem, the spectators greeted him with such great gladness that the Pharisees appealed to Jesus to shut them up. But he can't and he won't because "if they're silent, the very rocks would cry out."[2] Yes, this is hyperbole, this is mystery too deep for me, but of this I am sure: God speaks and all of creation answers back—in joy, in praise, in truth. That's what we're doing in this book. We're still naming the word-spoken world; we're writing the story of our life. We're answering back. Not just to ourselves and to God, but also to one another.

John, one of the men who followed Jesus, knew about this. He tells us in this opening to his letter exactly why he's writing:

That which was from the beginning, which we have heard, which we have seen with our eyes, which we have looked at and our hands have touched—this we proclaim concerning the Word of life. The life appeared; we have seen it and testify to it, and we proclaim to you the eternal life, which

was with the Father and has appeared to us. We proclaim
to you what we have seen and heard, *so that you also may
have fellowship with us. And our fellowship is with the Father
and with his Son, Jesus Christ. We write this to make our joy
complete.*

1 JOHN 1:1-4, EMPHASIS ADDED

John wrote, we're writing these things to you—what we've seen,
heard, touched, handled—to make our joy complete! Incredibly, it
wasn't enough to witness the life of Jesus among them. Their joy
wasn't complete without passing it on! And when they did this, a
new community was formed: Through the reading of these words,
we are drawn together, and together, we're drawn into fellowship
with the Father and Son.

Our own stories do no less. When we pass on our stories to one
another, we form a very real triangular community: We're drawn
into the presence and the hearts of one another, and together, we're
drawn closer to God. This is holy, holy work. Even for those who
are uncertain of God, shared words can profoundly move hearts
and join lives.

When Zandree wrote a scene in class about the doctor drilling
through her bone, she wrote surrounded by others who were also
writing deeply into their lives. Zandree noticed a shift as she wrote
her "showing" scene:

Leslie taught about scene and invited us to transform our
drafts into something our readers could see, hear, touch,
taste, and feel. When I did this, my relationship to that
moment of diagnosis shifted entirely. As I drafted the
experience for a second time, I no longer wrote for me;
I wrote for someone else out there who is living or has
lived her own moments of deep pain. I wrote to connect

to her heart, to walk with her through visceral pain with the goal of building healing community through mutual understanding of ourselves and God with us. Moving from writing for me alone to writing to invite others into shared experience gave that particular moment in my life, in all its horror, purpose in the world. The rendering of the horrific traumas in our lives for the purpose of birthing encouragement, fellowship, love, belonging, and a deeper communion with God brings a violent defeat of the enemy.

But the question arises: Who is our audience? Are we writing only for those who share our beliefs or disbeliefs, who wear the same shade of choir robes as we do, or who dress in the same tint of doubt? We cannot cloister or limit ourselves this way. We want to hear from others along their own winding paths, don't we, no matter how different from our own? And don't we hope that others will want to hear from us? I hope we'll make room, then, and write in such a way that all can enter into our words, our disappointments, the day the doctor said, "I'm sorry, but it's cancer." The day your daughter won the marathon, the week your son got divorced. We have so much common human ground, let's come together to form the best kind of gathering I know: a gathering of differents, a community of strangers who become, soon, a trusted circle of friends.

At the end of this chapter, I'll introduce you to LifeStory Circles and give you guidelines about forming them. I hope you can do this. I hope you can find others who will journey through this book with you.

Even as I say this, I know that some of you are not able to write and share your stories in community. Many of you reading this book are writing alone. Bless you, and keep writing. If you can find an audience, even just one other, as you write, you will be glad for it. If you cannot—and there have been long periods of my life when I could not—just keep writing. So much good is coming from your pen, your keyboard. And your words *will* find an audience at just the right time.

What if you join a LifeStory Circle, and then the worst thing happens? What if everyone in your class or circle is better than you? Of course they are! Every time I'm in a writing group I fall in love with everyone else's words and I feel my own wither in comparison. Don't you know others will fall in love with your words, too, and think their own are paltry and poor next to yours?

Let's stop doing this, comparing voices. Let's remember the real world we live in, which is a world abounding in gifts, voices, and experiences. Let's dump our culture's competitive mind-set where we rank and measure everything. It begins the moment we're born with our Apgar score, and soon, we're ranked and marked from kindergarten all the way through graduate school. Now we've gadgeted up our lives so we can measure and rank our steps, and even the few hours of our lives when we try to sleep! Can we put all that away? It's not real. The real world runs not on scarcity, not on competition, but on abundance.

On a January night in Kodiak, I was working on a book. It was 10:30 p.m. Tired, under a deadline, and riddled with doubt, I knew I needed to go to bed, but I wanted to finish the chapter. While working, I glanced at my Facebook feed and discovered that the northern lights were ablaze. I was missing too much life. I shut my computer, proclaimed a "Northern Lights Search Party," and yanked my sons out of bed. (They were both still awake, reading sneakily by flashlight.)

We jumped into the car in various states of dishabille and drove to the top of a mountain, up a switchback road, passing—count them!—thirty cars on the narrow gravel passage coming down. The whole town was out!

At the top of the mountain, beneath massive windmills, we

scoured the black horizon for the shimmering waves of light—but saw only blackness, and then, something else. As our eyes shifted to night mode, they appeared, faint at first, then growing in intensity until we all gasped—a swimming sea of stars, like the night ocean alive with phosphorescence. We bathed in their glory together for a long moment while three windmills strong-armed the sky overhead.

I was under a book deadline. I am so aware of my limitations, how others' words and stories are often so much better than mine. How can I compete? How can my words ever make it among so many brighter lights? But standing there, I realized something. There is no single star that knocks us down. It is the panoply of stars that take our breath. It is the uncountable collectivity of galaxies and star clusters that light the black sky and plow us down into worship and humility. It is their sheer density and magnitude that teach us our size and then make us glad to be small.

Yes, I am small. Dear friends, aren't we all small? Each of us is one among millions of talented, smart, creative others and their stories. Lucky us—we get to hear and listen and learn from them all. Write your stories for all of us. Keep going. You're already a star. Now you get to join a constellation.

Your Turn!

This chapter ends with *your* stories rather than others'. We're practicing a skill crucial for every writer—*and* every human being: the art of listening well to one another.

1. What has been your experience with out-loud storytelling or reading? (In Kodiak, we have "Galley Tables," where seven people tell a story in seven minutes on a particular theme.[3]

WHAT IS A LIFESTORY CIRCLE?

A LifeStory Circle is simply a group of people sharing their writing together. The circle can be as few as two and as many as eight, depending on the time, the need, and the story. The ideal size is often three to five people.

Why a LifeStory Circle?

Sharing our stories

- **moves us** from isolation and individualism to our truest state: belonging to the human community and the whole body of Christ.
- **strengthens us** to break chains that bind us and to overcome the cyclical burdens of our past.
- **brings comfort and encouragement** to one another, allowing us to "rejoice with those who rejoice, weep with those who weep."[4]
- **declares God's glory:** "Declare his glory among the nations, his marvelous works among all the peoples!"[5]
- **builds up the church:** "What then shall we say, brothers? When you come together, everyone has a hymn or a teaching, a revelation, a tongue, or an interpretation. All of these must be done to build up the church."[6]

Half the town shows up for these.) Why do you think hearing stories aloud is so moving and powerful?

2. What are some reasons we might hesitate to share our stories with one another? Talk together about some of these fears and hesitations. How does this chapter help alleviate some of those concerns?

LifeStory Circle Guidelines: Be R.E.A.L.*

1. **Recognize** that it's a privilege to be entrusted with others' stories. Listen with gratitude and full attention.

2. **Enough time:** Designate a timekeeper in each group. Example: If you've got thirty minutes for sharing, the timekeeper can manage the time so that each one in the group has enough time to read.

3. **Always be affirming.** Respond as friends and human beings first, not as editors, judges, or critics. We don't have to like or agree with a story to be supportive of the writer. Our role is to be witnesses and encouragers.

4. **Let the writer take the lead** in requesting feedback. Sometimes feedback isn't desired and the writer just needs listeners. Other times writers want feedback. Here are some questions the writer could ask of the listeners:

- Is there any part that was confusing?
- Is there any part I should develop more? Or any part that doesn't feel relevant to the story?
- Do I have enough scenes/summary/reflection?

* **Important Note:** LifeStory Circles are not a substitute for therapy or professional help. If you have traumas you need to work through, please seek appropriate professional guidance.

3. It's your turn now to enjoy what I believe will soon be your favorite part of this book. Those of you going solo, hold on. I have something for you as well!

- If you're working through this book with friends or in a class, form a LifeStory Circle (or circles, depending on how many are in your class). Pull out the scenes you wrote in the last chapter or your encounter-with-God story. Choose the piece you'd most like to share. Take turns reading and responding around the circle, following the guidelines given above. Be sure to let everyone read who desires to.

- You may be working through this book in an online book club, or with friends who live in other cities. Consider other ways of reading your work aloud to one another: through Facebook Live, Zoom, or Skype, for example. Reading your words aloud and hearing others' words, even through a screen, can still be powerful.

- If you're reading and writing solo—first, kudos to you for knowing the importance of this work and doing it on your own! But I'd also love for you to cultivate a reader or two, if possible. Is there someone in your life, perhaps a trusted friend, who might enjoy some of your work and who would encourage more than critique? Ask them and see. Maybe it's your son or daughter. Or your next-door neighbor. Or perhaps you have a childhood friend that you keep track of through Facebook. Sending one or two short pieces a week to them could be an encouragement to you and a blessing to them.

- This last category is for me, for all the years I wrote completely alone, and for those of you here without a group or reader to share with. You're not alone! You're here in these pages with a whole host of us sharing our stories. Here's something valuable that you can do: As you write your stories after each chapter, try reading them aloud, giving them your full voice. You'll experience your words differently out loud than on the page. Consider recording it as well. You'll get a whole new sense of the value and meaning of your story when you hear it aloud. (*And* you'll be creating a valuable audio record of your life, faith, and thoughts.)

CHAPTER FIVE

YOUR INNER STORY

Reflecting

*I know my gift is limited. I know I cannot stand toe to toe with philosophers
or theologians nor solve for myself or anyone else the problems of evil, either
natural or moral. But we who are writers can tell a story, or write a poem.
Where rational argument will always fail, somehow, miraculously in metaphor
and simile and image and simple narrative, there is both healing
and illumination. We write stories not because we have
answers but because we have questions.*

KATHERINE PATERSON, IN *SHOUTS AND WHISPERS:
21 WRITERS SPEAK ABOUT THEIR WRITING AND THEIR FAITH*

IT'S THE FOURTH WEEK OF CLASS, a yearlong Writing Life Stories class that's part of a larger university program. I watch everyone drift in, happy, chatting. I smile at Jack, nod at Cherry. "Hey, Russell." "Come on in, Lisa." There are fourteen in this evening class. I'm pleased with the community that's already formed. But I have a small pit of dread in my stomach tonight. Two people submitted their stories for our feedback. One is marvelous. The other is—not.

"Okay, everyone, we've got tons to do! I'm going to talk about scenes tonight. We'll do some writing and sharing. And in the last hour, we're going to look at two more stories—David's and Jeanna's, right?" I smile widely at both as they give me fake terrified smiles back.

At first, the class goes well. I am pleased with everyone's engagement with scenes. And the LifeStory Circle around David's story goes beautifully. The piece needs lots of work, but everyone is enthralled with his experience at the Sturgis Motorcycle Rally. Motorcycles always win in a writing class.

Now it's Jeanna's turn. She's somewhere in her fifties, I'm guessing. She's wearing a denim jacket and hoop earrings tonight. She looks confident.

"Okay, everyone. Let's take out Jeanna's piece. What did you like about this story?" I look around, eagerly, hoping someone will help me out here. Jeanna's story is about three of her ex-husbands and one of her former boyfriends. I don't think she's married right now. The story is funny. It is graphic. And it is mean. It would be a perfect contribution to an anthology for man-haters.

I look hopefully at Suzanne and Cathy, my "regulars" who often bail me out when I talk myself into a corner. Their heads are down, looking intently at their copy of the story. I glance around the semicircle. Everyone's avoiding eye contact.

Finally Jeanna breaks the silence. "Hey, guys, what's up? I'm just telling the truth about these so-called men," Jeanna says in a low, husky voice, looking around the room, annoyed now.

"Well, I'll start!" I blurt. I thought of one thing I can say. "Jeanna, I love that you're writing about important things. Relationships, of course, are good terrain for exploration."

"Oh yeah." She laughs. "I got tons more where that came from." She reaches under her chair and brings out an inch-thick manuscript and plops it down on her desktop. "This is it, my memoir. I'm just about done. That's the second chapter I gave you."

We sit, stunned.

"Wow, that's impressive," I finally say.

"How many pages is that?" Cathy asks.

"Two hundred and thirty-eight."

"How long have you been working on that?" I ask.

"Five years," she answers, proud. "It's about growing up in the Deep South during the race riots. And it's got a bunch more dirt on those fleabag husbands of mine." She looks delighted.

The class falls silent again. Everyone is looking at me. This is when I wish I were a butterfly scientist or a professional organizer of closets. Or a mortician. Why didn't I stick to just writing? Why didn't I listen to that professor who said writing can't be taught?

"Ummmm, Jeanna, I wonder if I may ask, ummmm, why did you take this class? It looks like you've already finished your memoir." I try to keep my voice light.

"I thought you could help me clean it up. You know, proofreading stuff, better words, more description, whatever. I'm happy with what I wrote. I want people to know about these so-called men." Her voice drops again on this last phrase.

Everyone is staring at me wide-eyed, wondering what I'm going to say. I'm wondering too.

"Soooooooo, I think this class is more about creating new writing, Jeanna, rather than bringing in what we feel is already finished," I venture cautiously. "While you're in this class, I'd really like for you to write some new material. And to practice the things we've been learning: scenes, and ummm, especially *reflection*." I emphasize this last word. I can't help it. I add a smile, looking around for backup.

Last week in class, I talked about the importance of reflection, about writing away from what we think we know, toward new understanding. We write not just from who we were *then* but from who we are *now*. The chapter she gave us to read was mostly a rant, all set in the past. The whole book sounds like a revenge chronicle.

Will raised his finger tentatively. "I gotta be honest with you, Jeanna. I like you. I think you've got a great sense of humor. But I wouldn't read very far into your book. You're kinda angry in this story. Are you like that all the way through?"

I am silently thanking God for honest men when Russell, who is in his seventies and rarely speaks, chimes in. "I don't think you like men very much."

"Oh, I like 'em, all right. That's why I keep marrying 'em!"

Jeanna cracks, and suddenly we laugh, relieved, all of us falling gratefully into this opening.

This chapter is for Jeanna and all of us who have written our stories already, and for those of us who are still just starting. We're onto the final and the most ground-shaking element of story-telling: reflection.

You've been writing scenes since chapter 3, and I hope you love it. I hope you've seen how scene literally lifts memories from the dust, raising them to corporeal life. But there's always a deeper question beyond the events we're resuscitating. Scene details the outer story, but there's an equally fascinating inner story. Sometimes we don't see it on our own. Often fellow writers in our LifeStory Circles can ask questions and help point us deeper.

I didn't have a class or any kind of story circle, but I did have Kate. I'm on the phone again with her now, a month after I finished those scenes in the fishing boat.

"Leslie, good scenes here. Graphic. Compelling." Her voice is clipped, hurried, as usual. "The book feels closer. But there's something crucial missing."

I've heard those words before. "What is it?" I ask with dread, wondering if she's going to tell me to scrap the whole thing and start over.

"Why did you stay? With all that happened, why didn't you jump ship and leave the island? That's what most people would have done. Why are you still there?"

I am silent. I didn't expect this. I feel like she's judging me, calling my whole life into question. I don't know how to answer. Then Kate breaks the silence.

"Well, the reader has to get it. I understand why you went into the Alaska wilderness, all that. But what kept you? And how were you changed at the end? Without that arc, there's no story."

"Yeah, okay," I say, heart sinking. I know Kate is talking about the inner story. Haven't I taught this to my students? Every story has at least those two layers: the outer story, what happens in the out-there world; and the inner story, the deeper story, the psychic, emotional, spiritual story. The outer story takes us into the past with scene and summary; the inner story—that searching, reflecting voice—is usually set in the present.

It's so tempting to stay in the past, to keep events safely distant. I wanted to do that. My students have as well. I had one student, Dan, who persistently wrote from his childhood in a child's voice. He resisted growing up and adding his adult perspective now. But why are we bothering to turn around and write behind us if not to write ourselves forward?

Yes, we're writing in pursuit of events and life stories that happened fifty years ago, or thirty years, or seven years. But that story set in the past is not complete without the story of the present. Your story is not just the thing that happened then but how you understand it now. You're a different person now than you were when your father lost his job and you and your siblings moved to a trailer in the desert. The best life stories, the most powerful memoirs, offer this dual lens: what happened in the past and how our present reckons with that past. The most compelling parts of our story are often this "story of thought."

No matter what the story is or where it takes place, you can't end up in the same place you started. A story must move us, both as writer and reader. That is, it must quite literally take us from one place to another: from the past to the present. From event to reflection. From ignorance to wisdom. From innocence to experience. Every story is a quest of sorts, and that quest often begins with a question. It must be a question that matters deeply to the writer, and it's the writer's job to make it matter to the reader as well.

If nothing happens or changes, there is no story. Yes, there are exceptions and experiments, such as French absurdist Samuel

Beckett's famous play *Waiting for Godot* and Jean-Paul Sartre's *No Exit*, where the characters are trapped in a state of misery and stasis with no possibility of change or resolution. Both plays end as hopelessly as they begin.

Postmodernism has spawned a host of such stories layered with irony: Look, a story told in three voices about an existentialist lying on his futon, smoking cigarettes, ruminating about an existentialist on his futon! These antistories are fascinating at first, revelatory of another worldview and the reality of some people's lives, but they often do not move or sustain. And ultimately, I believe, they do not tell the whole truth.

And here it is—theology again. Theology and story are never far removed from each other. What we believe about human existence, meaning, and the nature of time is fundamental to our storytelling. I am a hopeless optimist who believes this whole cosmic ball of wax is actually headed somewhere. That events are not random and without meaning or purpose. That there is value in asking questions, in tracing histories, in leaning close to learn from the past.

Writers in my classes have asked and written into all sorts of questions: *What happened to my father that night in the coal mine, and how did it affect our family? Why did I give up teaching, the one job I loved? Why did my mother start drinking? Where is home? Why did I leave the church? How did cancer change me?*

As we write into these questions, we move. If we're asking well, we move from ignorance toward understanding. And often, we move from the past into the present.* All of this movement creates the narrative arc.

I knew this before I began the memoir. This was the piece that scared me most about life stories and memoir. I wrote essays for years before attempting my own life stories. Essays could ramble

---

*But not always. If we're writing someone else's life story, we'll likely remain in the past, since the story is less about who they are now and more about their life experiences in the past.

anywhere you wanted. You could write about burning garbage on the beach, cutting up meat, building a house, watching bald eagles. All perfectly safe with no need to reflect and revise my own understanding of my life.

But how could I say no to this? I was committed. I had signed the contract. Somehow I knew that if I was going to grow as a writer and even as a person, I needed to take this next step. I was right. Writing life stories, and this particular piece of story-making—reflection—keeps changing my life. Again and again, with every book I write. And it will change yours.

I know that sounds over-the-top. But why do we write? We write to remember, to pass on some of what we've experienced in this life. Our families need to know where we've been and who we are. We can pass on hope as we share ways that we survived cancer, divorce, the loss of a spouse. All of this matters. But there is more. We write to find out what we don't yet know. We write now, from where we are in this stage of life, interrogating past stages. Who were we then? Who are we now? What wisdom have we found along the way? What wisdom might we find *now*?

There were questions I needed to ask: Who was that twenty-year-old girl, just married, standing in a skiff, trying to keep her balance in the new waters of marriage, living with her in-laws on a remote island in Alaska? Is there something here we all might see about finding and making a home in a strange land? I had written the outer stories of my life for ten years by then. But now, halfway through my life, thanks to a deadline and Kate's insistence, I wanted more. I wanted the inner story. I knew it didn't mean the inner story of my entire life. That was too overwhelming and impossible. I was looking for the inner story of my new life in Alaska.

So I did it. I started writing inside each of the significant events: when I got lost, alone, in a boat in a winter squall. When I pried our frozen laundry off the outside clothesline. Whenever I had the chance, I scribbled. I free-associated, digging down layer by layer. Each word, each question felt like a prayer. I felt like Jacob in the Old Testament story, the man who wrestled an angel of God all through the night. Jacob had stolen his twin brother's inheritance. When Esau, the robbed brother, threatened to kill him, Jacob fled. And now, years later, Jacob stands alone on the banks of a river in the dark as his brother approaches. He's terrified by the arrival of his past and the sure accounting for his theft of Esau's blessing. But someone else showed up. (And—take note!—this is all written as a scene!)

> That night Jacob got up and took his two wives, his two female servants and his eleven sons and crossed the ford of the Jabbok. After he had sent them across the stream, he sent over all his possessions. So Jacob was left alone, and a man wrestled with him till daybreak. When the man saw that he could not overpower him, he touched the socket of Jacob's hip so that his hip was wrenched as he wrestled with the man. Then the man said, "Let me go, for it is daybreak."
>
> But Jacob replied, "I will not let you go unless you bless me."
>
> The man asked him, "What is your name?"
>
> "Jacob," he answered.
>
> Then the man said, "Your name will no longer be Jacob, but Israel, because you have struggled with God and with humans and have overcome."
>
> Jacob said, "Please tell me your name."
>
> But he replied, "Why do you ask my name?" Then he blessed him there.
>
> So Jacob called the place Peniel, saying, "It is because I saw God face to face, and yet my life was spared."

The sun rose above him as he passed Peniel, and he was limping because of his hip.

GENESIS 32:22-31

This is a conversion story, a turning-point event that changed the course of Jacob's life. He was met by his past, and though frightened, he didn't flee. He leaned low and grabbed hold of his opponent however he could through that long night. It changed his future, marking the beginning of the nation of Israel (which means "he wrestles with God"). I wonder how many times, how many hours over the unfolding decades of his life, Jacob pondered the events of that night, rubbing his sore hip.

Jacob's story is real, I believe, but it's also a grand metaphor for what we're doing when we write. We can lay out all the events of our lives and present them in vivid scenes, with summary between to fill in the lesser spots, but our story is so much more than the outer events. We go out onto that white page, like Jacob on the plains beyond the river, to meet our past. And maybe we go with fear, not knowing who will come and what his intentions are. We wrestle with words. We wrestle to understand. To find wisdom. To find out our true name.

One of the biggest misconceptions about writers is that they sit around and think up Important Literary Things and that when they're done, they sit down to spill out all their genius on paper. The real truth? I know gaggles of writers, and we all write not because we have a grip on our own lives and know Important Things but because we *don't*. We write to find out Important Things. We write to fight against forgetting. We write to excavate. We write to discover that inner story, and it comes mostly through wrestling. Sometimes maybe we're grappling with an angel. Sometimes ourselves. Sometimes maybe even God.

I know this all sounds too mystical and too hard. How do

we actually do this? Let me show you a way: through a writing exercise I call WordSeeking. This practice is commonly known as Freewriting, but I'm renaming it to something I believe is more accurate. When we WordSeek, we're using words in pursuit of words, of course, but we're not recording thoughts, memories, and images as much as we're seeking. We're actively seeking memories,

A FEW WORDS ABOUT WORDSEEKING

What is WordSeeking?

It's the process of writing rapidly without stopping to edit or censor your words in any way. It trains the creative side of the brain to work freely, without interruption from the editing side of the brain. As we write inward to our deepest selves, seeking memory, wisdom, and understanding, we're also accessing the spiritual realm. What are we after? The *inner* story.

How do I do it?

- Warm up for a WordSeek by looking at photographs of the person/event you're writing about, or by reading their letters or talking about that person/event with someone.
- Write using the fastest, most comfortable method of getting words on the page. For most, this will mean using a computer. Others may prefer longhand (or shorthand) on a pad of paper.
- Don't write about just "anything." Choose a particular topic or event you want to explore. Here are two effective writing prompts:

  1. "For once, I want to tell the truth about _____ (*that night; the accident; leaving college . . .*)."

truth, and understanding. Jesus (who is also known as the Word), gives this invitation to all of us:

> Ask and it will be given to you; seek and you will find; knock and the door will be opened to you.
>
> MATTHEW 7:7; LUKE 11:9

2. "Remembering [this event] is important to me because
_____."

- To begin, use a timer. Start with just ten minutes at a time. Gradually increase, so that you're able to write freely for as long as twenty to thirty minutes. DO NOT STOP TO EDIT YOUR WORK. You can do that later.
- When you're done, read over what you've written with a highlighter or pen in hand. Highlight any paragraphs, phrases, and words that spark interest or new insight.
- The more you WordSeek before you write a story, the deeper and further the story will go. (Sometimes I WordSeek for a week before I settle on the direction of a story.)

Why should I invest so much time in this exercise?

WordSeeking may feel like it's undoing all your English teachers' insistence on correct diction, sentence structure, grammar, and punctuation, but it's not. That portion of your language and editing skills will remain intact, while your ability to access memories and to reflect meaningfully on them will grow exponentially. Through WordSeeking first, then editing, you're using *all* your resources: both sides of the brain *and* the Spirit.

This is just what we're doing: asking, seeking, knocking—using the tools given to us: words. And when we do this, we're somehow touching the divine.

When I teach people how to write stories from their lives, this part is always the roughest: convincing them to throw out their inner editor and just write like a river into their questions with no stops, no fixes, no backing up, just flowing wherever the water wants to go. It doesn't sound quite right, somehow, throwing out all the usual rules like that. It sounds like the start of anarchy, maybe, or like mysticism, or maybe even a little bit of socialism. You know, something threatening.

Jeanna was the most resistant to WordSeeking. A few weeks after our initial kerfuffle, I prepped the class to begin their first attempt. It went like this.

"Okay, I'm going to show you why we need WordSeeking. I'm going to start writing a story." I'm standing in front of a whiteboard with a blue marker in my hand. I scrawl across the whiteboard,

It was a dark and stormy night.

I stand back, regarding my genius words. "Oh, that's ridiculous. Such a cliché." I cross it out. "But wait, it *was* a dark and stormy night. No . . ." I cross out *stormy*. I try out a few other adjectives, then reverse the order of the adjectives. Then I realize, out loud, with the marker in my hand as I'm writing, that "Wait, no, it wasn't actually night. I think it was more like early evening." I cross out "night." And on I go for another thirty seconds, writing and rewriting until the whiteboard is filled with indecipherable cross-outs and arrows. I've managed to decide on two words: "nasty" and "evening." And I'm not even sure about those.

"Have you been spying on me?" David asks.

"Oh my gosh. That's my problem exactly," Amy says, looking as though I'd slapped her.

"Right!" I say, trying not to sound triumphant. "Do you all

see what's happening? My over-zealous editor keeps shutting me down. I can't get past the first sentence. If I stayed there, submitting every word to the scrutiny of my hypertensive editor, I'd never finish a chapter, let alone an entire book."

"I just want to write one story, and I can't ever get past the first paragraph," Cathy complains.

"I know. And neither could I. That's because Mrs. Lynchpin, our seventh-grade English teacher, did her job well! She and her offspring, the Guardians of the English Language, only want authority and perfection. They don't want to see your ideas. Or brainstorming. Or experiments. Or creativity. Or messy memories. And they certainly don't want to see any wrestling, holy or unholy, going on in the classroom!"

I know I'm getting a bit overexcited as I survey the faces in front of me. Rick is fixing me with a dubious stare. Shelley is looking at her hands. Cathy has a slight frown. I know they don't believe me.

"So—we have to trick her. Here's what we do. We lure her into the library, set out the *Oxford English Dictionary* in front of her, and lock the door on our way out. We're not being cruel. She'll be happily sighing as she pores over the pages with a magnifying glass. Now we're safe. Now the writer, the remember-er, the creator can move freely through memory, words, ideas, without concern for grammar, sentence structure, diction, or those pesky dangling modifiers. We're free! None of that matters right now because we're off WordSeeking."

"And what are we looking for, again?" asks Jeanna, looking resistant still.

"This leads us into reflection, the inner story, remember? I can't tell you what your inner story is, or the questions you need to ask. That's for you to decide. Are you ready to give it a try?" Everyone's eyes are on mine with varying degrees of doubt. If I were a cheerleader, this is the exact moment I'd leap, kick, and shake my pom-poms.

"Okay, so let's do this. Last week, we read about the valley of bones. Some of you started some excellent scenes around the word *bone*. Feel free to WordSeek into that. And today we read about Jacob and his night of fear. So here's a writing prompt if you want to WordSeek into that: *For once, I want to tell the truth about the night I was so scared.* Shall we try it? I'm setting the timer. Ten minutes. That's all we're going to do. Ready, go!"

And they're off. Everyone is writing, head down. A few glance nervously up at me, as if I'm going to rap them on their knuckles for pausing for breath. I watch them, I watch the clock, I write a few sentences myself. Then it's time.

"Okay, that's it! Ten minutes. Go ahead and finish your sentence or your paragraph. Just come to whatever closure you need."

Some throw their pens down with relief. Others are reading their words silently. I see surprise on a few faces.

We share our pieces with one another. Some in pairs, others in smaller groups.

Amy Zerger writes this:

Sinewy meat glistened in the moonlight, skulls, raw ribcages, leg bones. The wolves were naked, skinned and stacked on the trail. My trail. The shortcut through the graveyard that lead to one of only two main roads in my village---thick tongues lolling. To my nine year old mind icy bodies threatened supernatural resurrection. Go back? It's a 10 minute run through the woods to the nearest road. Snow crunches under my shifting feet and somehow this becomes a metaphor for my life. The monster in the trail, that thing that would stop me in my tracks and cause me to go back, running swiftly away from where I am meant to be. I am a middle child, I have never been brave. I have four older siblings for that. But today I am alone, it is decision time. Shoulders high sucking sharp wintery air into my lungs I race on.

Amy grew up in McGrath, Alaska, a remote village. She's never written like this before. She tells me later what this experience was like for her:

> That was hard. That perfectionist was really anchoring me. Once I got past the grip of the editor and allowed myself to tell the story, allowed myself to be imperfect, it was really freeing. I could just throw some words out there and not worry if they were the perfect words, not worry about punctuation, cadence. It was just about getting the story out there. And I realized I can go back later and fix that, perfect that. That's really freeing. It felt really good.
>
> Now when I'm bogged down, I turn to WordSeeking. In the moment it doesn't look like much of anything, but I leave it for a day and come back and then ohhhh— there's a start of an idea.

Even in that first ten-minute WordSeek in class, Amy found an aha moment.

> They had bounties out on wolves because there were so many. The hunters would throw the carcass wherever. Running along the trail at night, I would come upon them. I was just writing about that incident. Then I started thinking about this in a larger context. There have been lots of instances of being stopped in my tracks

because of a monster in the way. My lack of courage caused me to turn away and run back. I realized that I was listening to voices other than God. I had to really just trust and have faith and believe in God's provision and courage. He would do it for me. I really just had to follow. This was powerful for me.

You have to get in that cupboard and rattle those pans. You have to go out onto the empty plain, to the white screen. And whoever comes to meet you, you have to lean low, grab hard, and not let go. You have to be willing to question. Write beyond clichés that catch us unaware. Reach for as deep a truth as you can find. Be fearless. What are we creating here? We're not after good writing right now. We're after memory, we're after understanding, we're after reflection, the inner story.

And understand—we're not writing to convert anyone to our point of view, whatever it is. We're after the inner story. We're after true stories written as deeply and beautifully as we're able. In my own memoir, it was easy to remember this since I was writing for a general market. This reality released me from the grip of my zealous inner evangelist. She already had her way in my early poetry and in a novel I wrote just out of college, a flimsy allegory meant to drop us all to our knees in repentance. (It was horrendous writing, and no one dropped but me.) Somewhere along the crooked path of my faith, I came to understand that I don't need to "make" my work Christian. For those of us writing out of our Christian faith, we don't change an ending or add Bible verses to convert either our art or our readers. It's not our job to bring about redemption from our stories. We don't redeem our stories, our lives; God does. Our job is to tell the truth, to simply write from who we are, from where we've been, and we trust God for the rest. Jacques Maritain, the French Catholic philosopher, said it most clearly:

> If you want to make a Christian work, then *be* Christian, and simply try to make a beautiful work, into which your heart will pass; do not try to "make Christian." . . .
>
> But apply only the artist to the work; precisely because the artist and the Christian are one, the work will derive wholly from each of them.[1]

As we WordSeek into the past, into our deepest questions, we'll make noise. We'll fatigue our muscles. This is what we've come to do. Not simply to record the events of our lives: Here's where we were born, where we grew up. Here's what happened in school, in my marriage. Here are my jobs, my kids. All of that matters! Time and place and the concrete details of our lives matter. Our outer stories matter, but if we don't dig into them and do some holy wrestling, we'll miss the inner story, which is the better story.

WordSeek into as many scenes and moments as you can. If you're a Christian, peel back those words we use far too often as a kind of shorthand: redemption, grace, community, blessing. Stepping away from our normal way of speaking and processing takes practice. We're far more practiced using our words to proclaim, to announce, to declare our knowledge and our certainty. Now we're using words to ask, to question, to excavate, to listen. As seekers of God, isn't this a worthy use of our words?

Don't worry about making a mess. In fact, that is your job right now. We'll clean it up in later chapters, when we find out what we've come to say.

As for me and my story, I didn't know yet what I had come to say, even after so many months of writing.

"Why didn't you leave the island?" Kate had asked. I did leave. But I hadn't told that part of the story. I was afraid to. And now I knew I must, that this was key to the inner story of the whole book. I did it. Through WordSeeking, I went back to those days in the skiff, the long hours, the storms, getting sick and still needing to work, to the icy silences between Duncan and me, to the day I jammed clothes and food into a backpack and escaped the only way possible: by marching off the island to an empty shack made of driftwood, four miles down a bouldered beach, gun over my shoulder for bears. I did leave.

It was scary to call all that back. Even writing eighteen years after that difficult summer, I spilled out pages and pages. But in the midst of the mess, I slowly discovered that the story was different from what I thought it was. I began to discover truths I had never spoken. I began to feel less like a victim through some of the events. Somewhere in this process, I knew the old title had to go. *Awake on the Island of Listen* didn't work anymore. This was not a story of passive observation: This was a story of agency and survival. The new title had to have that word in it. I didn't know what else yet, but it was clearly about body-and-soul survival. I still had much to sort through, but I was getting closer.

Ask, seek, and knock—and the door will open to a deeper story than you knew.

Your Turn!

1. Read the two essays at the end of this chapter: "When Arms Fail" and "Ow, You're Hurting Me!" Both work to move past appearances to challenge earlier assumptions. What deeper truths did the writers discover?

2. Now you get to do your own WordSeeking, which will
lead you into that inner story: the reason you write, and
the reason we read. Don't forget what we're after. We're not
after good writing right now. We're after memory, we're after
reflection, we're after the inner story.

   a. Look at the scenes you wrote from the last chapter.
   Choose one that pulls at you still. You know there's more
   to explore. Use this prompt to WordSeek into the heart of
   that event:

   For once, *I want to tell the truth about the day
   that* _____.

   Set a timer for twelve minutes. Remember to keep
   writing, to not stop to edit or change what you've written.
   This helps us learn to write, remember, and seek freely
   without our editor leaning over our shoulder, shutting us
   down. It's going to be messy and fun!

   b. When the WordSeek is done, catch your breath, shake
   out your hands, and then read it, silently or aloud. Nearly
   every WordSeek yields at least one reflective "treasure,"
   which may become the key to your inner story. Underline
   or circle any word, phrase, sentence, or idea that buzzes,
   hums, or tinkles like wind chimes as you read it.

   c. Let's go one more time! You've found a treasure. Now
   let's open it! Do one more WordSeek into that key idea
   or phrase, whatever you found in the first WordSeek.
   Go again for twelve minutes, if you can. These treasures,
   ideas, will help you form the inner story for each of the
   stories you write.

3. In your LifeStory Circles, take turns sharing about the experience of WordSeeking. Did you find this exercise easy or difficult? Why? Share some of the insights you gained from the first and second WordSeeks.

Try to do at least one WordSeek every day. Remember to mine the treasure after each one. You might increase the time each day by a minute. You'll be surprised at how your capacity to remember, to reflect, and to write freely without your inner editor grows each time.

WHEN ARMS FAIL

By Tony Woodlief

It is darkest night, and it is the last night my four children will ever go to sleep thinking their mother and father will always be married. Tomorrow we tell them it's not to be that way.

My heart quails at the thought of what we have planned, how it would be better to slap each of them full in the face. An unbroken home is something we swore we would give them, no matter the cost, no matter the cost.

Some costs can't be borne. In bearing them, you inflict pain on the very ones you claim to love. This is what we tell ourselves, at least, and I think sometimes it is true, though I can't explain, anymore, why we are divorcing.

I know the reasons, the deeply hurtful, personal reasons. But I can't string them into a narrative that makes sense. When I try to set them down piece by piece, the way a lawyer might forge an argument, say, or a bricklayer might plant his path in scored earth, I lose my way.

I can't explain why the burdens are too great now. Two years ago, they were not. They were not even too great in the second before we wept and agreed to dissolve what we swore to uphold. Some days, I think we decided to divorce because we must; other days, I think we must divorce because it is what we decided.

Sometimes I think we are doing it because we each of us came to the brink one night, and neither of us blinked. No marriage survives if nobody blinks. Is that all this is? Two souls too weary to fear the abyss?

All I know to tell my children is that sometimes you get a wound, and if you scrape that wound every day, it will never heal. This is your mother's heart, I will tell them. I'll insist that they will see me every bit as often as they do now. This is the silver lining in my work commute. We have already lived in quiet separation for a year, disguised by my job. Someone said absence makes the heart grow fonder. Someone said this.

I will explain to those four upturned faces that we love them, that we love them more than ourselves. But already, those unspoken words sound hollow. We are either too stubborn or too weak or too angry to give them this gift we swore to give them. Don't we love them enough? Don't we?

I haven't been able to focus on anything, for very long, in months. The last chapters of a novel remain unedited. I forget, on planes, where it is I am going. I lose entire paragraphs in conversations and can only nod, and smile, and work to keep the tightness in my stomach like stone, because to let in food or air will only soften it and then I will vomit or scream or both.

My babies, I keep thinking to myself. *My babies. What will happen to my babies?*

I try to remind myself that the messed-up kids of divorce are being raised by messed-up parents who got divorced because they are messed-up. It's a spurious causation, I insist. But then, I am a lot messed up, and their mother at least a little.

And now they see that a love can dissolve, that people who

love each other and live together can undo their bond. What great insecurity will this unleash in their hearts? *My babies.*

There is no prayer that gives comfort, no bottle that brings enough forgetfulness. I drink too much, and I rage at the night, and still nothing will change the reality that the two of us together cause more harm than good to one another's souls. What damage does a soul-weary parent do to a child? How much more or less is this damage than the harm of divorce? What dread mathematician knows the answers?

Some people tell us not to do this, and others say they are not surprised, and others look at us like someone they love has died.

I return to math, to statistics, to the consolation that most people who have buried their children don't last. People will forgive us, I think. They have to forgive us. Even our children have to forgive us, don't they?

Letting myself be forgiven, feel forgiven—that's another mystery entirely.

I used to think it was an exaggeration, the depiction of a parent throwing out his arm, in a braking car, to catch his forward-lurching child. Then one day in the rain I hit my brakes and found my arm wrapped across my nine-year old's chest, because this is what you learn to do, you learn to catch them when they toddle and fall, to put your flesh between them and the hard point of impact.

How are you supposed to protect them when that impact is you?

OW, YOU'RE HURTING ME!

By Arthur Boers

"Ow, you're hurting me!" Her complaint carries through thin walls between their bedroom and mine.

These are the first words, the first sentence, I remember hearing as a child. I stand on my wobbly mattress, my flannel pyjamas covered with giraffes, dampened from sweaty sleep, my hair mussed. I clamber pudgy legs over the rail, slide my torso across, and lower myself to the hardwood. Then I run, out my room and into my parents', arms stretched high, crying "Superman!" I leap onto the double bed that almost fills their room, crawl over bunched sheets and rough woolen blankets and squirm between them. I push them apart to break up their grappling.

And they laugh at three-year-old me.

I become Superman over and over again. Years pass before I realize that my parents play me, colluding in my provocation, making early-morning noise to provoke my reaction. They enjoy the pajama-clad toddler coming to the rescue. A great way to start the day.

My father is never gentle. When I or my sister hold a balloon, he touches it with lit cigarette or prods it with a sharp pencil, laughing as bright, flimsy spheres explode and we startle, even cry. I learn to stay away from him, on the far side of the room, especially on rare occasions when I have a balloon.

He wrestles with people weaker or smaller—my mother, younger relatives. Papa favors vice-grip headlocks, ear twisting, grinding knuckles into skulls. Once he scuffles with his cousin Art, five then, my dad twenty years older. He yanks Art's ear so hard that it partially detaches, begins bleeding, requires stitches. Relatives frequently tell this story, always with a laugh, but now I am horrified. Art, over seventy, still grins at the memory, but winces at the same time, and I feel shame. My father wrestles with me, from when I am a toddler until my adolescence. When I grow muscles enough to compete my father stops, disappointing me, because I want the satisfaction of matching him or even winning at least once.

Over the years when he occasionally goes off course—drinking too much, smashing a car, exploding with expletives, pitching glass across a construction site as employees run for cover—my mother invites other males (her father, your father's uncle) to "talk to Paul." Papa straightens out for a time, but eventually another intervention is required. I, too, will be groomed for this role.

Except that now I wonder what this whole routine taught me about marital relations, about men's power over women, about inappropriate invitations into interventions. I always react, certain I do the right thing. It's classic: heroic rescuer delivers distressed damsel. King Arthur or shining-armored knight, a cowboy on his steed. I see enough television—*Robin Hood, Lone Ranger*—to know the scripts. And I keep replaying them in that small two-bedroom apartment.

And then I replay them in other ways in later years, as an activist and protester—against the politics of my father—and, still later, as a pastor who loves to rescue, loves to be needed, not understanding the hazards of such patterns.

*   *   *

Here is another toddler story.

A colorful Indonesian batik—brought back by my father from his overseas military stint, the one whose traumas haunted him with sweaty nightmares for the next four decades—drapes the wall above the gray couch. A wide ashtray collects my father's Buckingham butts atop a stand. The low pine coffee table bears a plant; greenery sprouts on the windowsills. Everything tickles my nose with faint cigarette staleness.

Then a clay-potted geranium wobbles through the air toward the four-by-four-foot living room window. Dirt drifts down onto the carpet during the flight. I see this without surprise.

As the geranium approaches, I see my mother move aside and

duck. The pot passes and strikes the pane. The impact reverber-
ates like a tinkling cymbal, the surface giving a little and then
cracking, spidering in all directions. The splinters hail down
inside and outside onto the lawn two stories below. Large shards
drop from the frame, some impaling themselves into the hardwood and the lawn. Others shatter as they fall against the sill,
the floor, the ground. The plant flies on in its alfresco arc, before
dropping from sight.

When all the objects stop moving and the glass stops falling,
the room is silent. Then I hear robins in trees and cars passing a
block away. I'm only three.

Picturing this today, I see my parents as I know them much
later, middle-aged and ought-to-know-better. Doing the math,
I realize that they are close to thirty. I could be the parent of
those troubled, immature youngsters. Yet at half my present
age, they already endured more trauma than I will ever know:
Depression childhoods; witnessing lives taken during the Nazi
Occupation; giving up everything in immigration; uprooting to
a foreign country where they could not speak the language. They
know about survival, but not the luxury of feelings, their own
or others'.

I now try to understand what went before. My father was frequently beaten by his father, assaults that included leather-booted
kicking. My grandmother fed my father early suppers and then
sent him to bed, before his father came home from work, to pre-
empt abuse. Perpetual fury moved hydraulically down through
generations and will focus on me.

* * *

He will die thirty years or so after he broke the window. I will think
I achieve peace with him. I never figure out how to ask about his

anger and realize that some gaps never get crossed. I love him and feel sure he loves me. I need nothing more.

One night early in that last May, my father has not spoken for thirty-six hours, his capacity gone. I insist that my mother, exhausted from caretaking, sleep in the guest room. I lie beside him all night in their bed. I help him to the bathroom and clean him, the first time I see him naked. I speak Dutch, hoping to console him. I expect this caregiving apprenticeship to last months.

But in the morning, my wife, a nurse, unexpectedly declares: "His circulation is shutting down; he's nearing the end." I grip his limp right hand, the one that hit me in fury more than once, the one scarred by his work with glass. Within the hour, his breath speeds but with less and less purchase. By lunch, he is gone. I think, hope, he finally has peace.

A few years later, I drive near his last home. I slow down past the place where we lived when I was a teenager. My father let loose there with fists and feet at fourteen-year-old me, knocking me down, and when I rose, knocking me down again, and finally pummeling me with apples that tumbled out of a ceramic fruit bowl that he smashed. I wander over to the red Insulbrick house that my family inhabited before that, the place where he battered seven-year-old me into a blackout.

Over the years, I will shock myself. I twice smash windows in anger, once in our garage and once in a shopping plaza. I will feel the tempting tug to tyrannize my children. I hope that the seeds of his rage no longer grow within me.

CHAPTER SIX

YOUR HEALING STORY

Understanding

The sad things that happened long ago will always remain part of who we are
just as the glad and gracious things will too, but instead of being a burden of
guilt, recrimination, and regret that make us constantly stumble as we go, even
the saddest things can become, once we have made peace with them, a source of
wisdom and strength for the journey that still lies ahead. It is through memory
that we are able to reclaim much of our lives that we have long since written off
by finding that in everything that has happened to us over the years God was
offering us possibilities of new life and healing which, though we may
have missed them at the time, we can still choose and be brought
to life by and healed by all these years later.

FREDERICK BUECHNER, *TELLING SECRETS*

ONE DAY DURING THE SUMMER, on Harvester Island, I got an email from a friend whose father had died. In her grief, aswirl with memories, she sent me the eulogy she had written for this kind, generous man. I didn't know her father, but I read her words with tears and a racing heart. In the space of a few pages, her words awakened a lifetime of suppressed confusion and anger toward my own father. I realized that when my father died, though I was a woman of words, I would have no words for him. Nor tears. Nor, likely, would anyone else. How could someone be born into this world, work, serve in the military, marry, father six children, live for eighty-some years, and leave this world without a tear to mark the loss?

I was writing about hard places in that first memoir, but I wrote as little as I could about people. How could I write well and fairly about living, breathing people around me who were *not* begging to be in my book? I was already on notice from one person. A few years before, when my first book came out, about women in commercial fishing, my mother stood me in front of her and said, in a commanding voice, eyes locked on mine, "Don't write about me until I'm dead."

"Oh, okay," I stammered, taken aback. I had no plans to do so.

But during the time I worked on the memoir, Kate asked about my mother. Did I have a mother? Why was she virtually absent in my writing? Kate kept complaining about the holes in my story without her. I could only say, "I can't write about her." In the two chapters about my growing-up years, I had to account for my parents in some way. So I included a few paragraphs about my father. I knew he'd never read my book and he likely wouldn't care. Did I dare to write anything further?

It's scary to write about other people, no matter how warm our relationships. Placing anyone on the page, even ourselves, always requires some kind of distortion. We can only present pieces, moments, a part of who they are, and even then, it's from our perspective only. How is this fair? Does anyone want to be flattened and examined on a two-dimensional page? Aren't we all fragile beings, stumbling through this crooked-path life, trying to do our best?

And yet. Much of the story and drama in our lives centers around family and difficult relationships. In class, when I ask, "How many of you have experienced difficult people?" some put their hand up slowly, tentatively, looking around warily for the family police. Some raise their hand partway, limp and weary, like a flag at half-mast. Several will shoot their hand up in fresh anger. But everyone raises a hand.

Then I ask, "How many of you have written about these strained relationships?" Most of the time, no one raises even a finger. (Except Jeanna, who could fairly raise both hands and a foot.) When I ask why, the reasons sound the same themes:

- *My father would kill me if he read this piece.*
- *If I write about what happened, my brother would never speak to me again.*
- *My mother thinks my childhood belongs to her. When I write anything about it, she calls me a liar.*
- *One time I wrote about something that happened to me and my sister. She remembered it totally differently and took offense.*
- *If I told the truth about my ex-husband, he'd sue me.*

Are we then consigned to silence around some of the most momentous and fascinating parts of our lives? How can we write into and out of our lives if we go mute when we most want and need to speak? What happened to the call to tell the truth?

When my friend's email first came, I didn't know the answer to these questions. I didn't know about the research. I only knew I had no choice. I knew intuitively that I had to venture out into the valley of bones with my father, searching for whatever words could be found. I decided to set aside the memoir (sorry, Kate—this is more important) and to write for myself alone, without any thought of publication.

Freed from that litany of fears, I began writing down every memory I had of my father. The list was scant. Then I broke each memory open into scenes, like the scenes we practiced in the first few chapters. I needed to return to those moments full-bodied and awake.

I remembered the moment I hugged him that day when he

was kicked out of the house. When he took me on a driving lesson in that old beat-up Mercedes on the potholed road we lived on. How he spent summer nights outside, smoking cigarettes and watching the sky for UFOs, which he believed in with all of his heart. The times my mother made him take off his belt and how he narrowed his lips as he whipped the backs of our legs again and again. How he drank Yuban instant coffee every morning and ate jello like he did in the army, with evaporated milk poured over the top. I remembered him out in the woods with the chain saw, helping us build a woodpile to warm us through the winter. Then my last memory: when I took all my kids to meet him in Florida for the first and only time.

I began to write. I began a story like this:

When my father dies, I may not know about it for days. The people at his housing complex in Sarasota, Florida, don't know that he has children—six, actually. He has not told anyone about this fact of his life. When he collapsed on the sidewalk last year, it was at least a week before I heard.

I am practicing now, writing about him, venturing out onto a vast empty plain, knowing that day is coming. He is eighty-six, I think, with diabetes, phlebitis, and smoker's lungs that heave his chest with every breath. We will not have a service. The cessation of his breath will not be enough to draw us together. No one would cry. I don't want to go to a funeral where no one cries.

Remembering, for me, felt like recovery work, like I was going after a drowning man. Or maybe a drowning woman. I thought of Patricia Hampl's words, about commemoration, her belief that "every life is sacred and that life is composed of details, of lost moments, of things that nobody cares about, including the people who are wounded or overjoyed by those moments." She goes on to say, "I don't think people allow themselves to value their lives enough. They ignore and discard these fragments."[1]

I was recovering these fragments, but they weren't enough, of course. The question beneath every scene I wrote wasn't answered. Why did my father seldom speak to me? Why didn't he care about anyone in his family? Why couldn't he hold a job? Why did he steal our money and leave? What was wrong with him?

My words came in a torrent of interrogation, hurt, and curiosity. But I soon hit a dead end. My memories, my experiences were not enough, I realized, because they were only mine. If I was committed to finding truth, I could not stop with the truths of my story; I had to discover the truths of his story as well.

I began to research mental illnesses. I interviewed his brother and sister-in-law, whom I hadn't spoken to since I was a teenager. I asked about his parents, whom I hadn't known. I asked my other siblings about their memories. I talked to mental-health experts. I got up early every morning for months and worked.

The larger story I unearthed about my father was not pretty, but it was a relief in many ways. I found a name for my father's condition. And more, I began to see that my father had not been loved. Yes, he abused others. The human damage is significant, and there is no excuse for that, but there was abuse in his own life as well. I began to see that my family and I were not the only ones lying on the side of the road, robbed and bleeding. He was lying there too.

As I wrote and wrestled, the most unexpected thing happened. After thirty years of little contact, the words that appeared under my pen sent me on a plane to Florida. They walked me into his nursing home, they set my hands on the handles of his wheelchair. They seated me beside him in an ice-cream parlor, sharing a bowl of vanilla ice cream with chocolate sauce. Two years later, after he died, those words sent me into the ocean.

One hot, oppressively humid afternoon, a brother, a sister, and I, the three of us, waded out into the ocean he loved and emptied his ashes from our Ziploc bags. We didn't have a funeral. No one would come. But we cried. The three of us cried.

The words I found to write about my father's life still were not done. They later sent me into prison.

* * *

I'm in a maximum-security prison in California, famous for over-crowding. We're in a supply closet ringed with shelves of prison uniforms and paper products. It was the only space they could find for our class. I'm sitting in a circle of folding chairs, nearly thigh to thigh with fifteen women wearing the same blue uniforms that are stacked behind us. They are all ages. They are blonde, dark-skinned, gray-haired, young, seniors, and they are all felons. The prison chaplain tells me beforehand that these women have found faith behind the razor wire. Some have even read the forgiveness book that tells my story with my father. When this workshop on forgiveness was offered, they were the first to sign up.

I start. "Hi, I'm Leslie. Would you all tell me your names before we start?"

"Hey, Leslie," the woman on my left calls out. "I'm Lucy. You got lipstick on your teeth." She points. "That's gonna bug the heck outta me."

"Yeah, that would bug me too." I use the sleeve of my sweater, then turn and bare my teeth at her. "Did I get it?"

"Nope. Still there."

I try again, then show her my teeth.

"That's good enough," she says.

It's a great start, the perfect equalizer. I begin telling some of my story with my father and something about forgiveness. They listen, then speak back, telling their stories of abuse, abandonment, violent husbands, mental illness, drugs, homelessness. We talk about the ways we lock our offenders in our own prisons, how exhausting it is for us to keep them there, and all the ways anger and hate destroy us. There are so many tears that someone reaches behind her to the shelf for a roll of toilet paper and we pass it, wiping our faces, one to the next. I don't know exactly why, but I feel at home with these women.

But talking isn't enough. I know if we're going to go deeper, we need to write. Writing always accesses a deeper well than our spoken words.

"Hey, everyone, looks like you all have journals or paper with you? I'd like us to do some writing."

They pull out their notebooks instantly.

"I'm hoping you came to this workshop with someone in mind, someone you know you need to forgive. Would you write down the name of that person?"

Everyone is done in about ten seconds. Clearly, they were ready.

"Okay, tell what happened between you—a short version. And be gut-honest about it. Maybe you had a fight one night. Maybe your ex left you all his debts. Tell the truth. Be angry if you want or need to. Write what happened and exactly how you felt. We'll take about five minutes."

The women lean into their pens, into their notebooks on their knees. I hear nothing but the sound of words shot onto paper.

I wait until they start slowing down. "Okay, so how did that feel?" The answers came rapid-fire. These women didn't waste time.

"It makes me freakin' mad all over again," says an older woman with reddish hair. "I'm in here because of him." The other women look at her and nod. They know her story.

"I know what happened. My mother still won't believe me. I just want her to know the truth," says a young woman with short blonde hair. I think her name is Lorie.

"The truth is the truth. Good, bad, we just gotta deal with it, you know?" says a young woman passionately.

"Yeah, you're exactly right," I say back. "Whatever happened, we want to face it, even when people do bad things. We have to call that out. That's our job. But there's another side to this. Didn't Jesus say some things about love?" I look around the circle, hoping I'm not switching gears too soon. I'm not a therapist; I'm not a pastor. Just a writer. Just a teacher. I hope that's enough.

One woman, Shanille, who kept her head down through most of the sharing, looks up at me for the first time and says softly, "Yeah. We're supposed to love God." She can't be more than twenty.

Lucy, next to me, says, "We got to love our neighbor. We just read that in a Bible study last week or month, whatever. We're supposed to love our enemies, too, but that ain't easy. Maybe it ain't even possible." Lucy told us earlier she had been sexually abused through most of her childhood.

"There's a bunch of Bible verses about forgiving like we've been forgiven, something like that," says a woman who said earlier she has six children.

"Yes," I reply. "So this is tricky. We need to tell the truth of our own experience, which you just did—but we're also asked to love and forgive. How do we do that? Anyone here know the Good Samaritan story?"

"Hey, I do," says a middle-aged woman with dark hair. "You want me to say it?"

I nod encouragingly.

She shifts in her seat and looks down at the floor as she speaks, her hands clasped in her lap. "So it's about a guy who gets beat up on his way from one city to another. I forget the cities. But these thugs steal everything he's got and leave him by the road to die. Three dudes come along, and they just ignore him, like they don't even see him, but they do. They just don't wanna be involved. And the thing is, one is like a priest, all religious, so he's supposed to help, but he doesn't. Then the last guy comes along . . . I can't remember who he is, but everyone hates him. And he turns out to be the one who helps the hurt dude." She looks up around the circle. "That's it, right?" she asks, looking at me.

"Wow, perfect," I say. "Okay, here's where I'm going with this. Maybe that's your story too? You got jumped and mugged along the way, along the way to wherever you were going. All of us did, in some way. There we are, lying on the ground, bleeding. But if we look over across the road, maybe we're going to see someone who really hurt us, lying over there beat up too. Yeah, we need to call out what he did, what she did. We need to tell the truth. But I hope maybe, through writing, we can find a larger perspective. You want to try?" I look around the circle. What if they say no? I have no backup plan.

"Yeah, I'll try," Judy says. "I know I'm locked up with that guy. I'm tired of hating him. It's like he's ruining my life twice."

"I forgave my mother," Jackie adds. "It made me feel so free."

"I'm not writing about my abuser. I can't forgive him. He's the demon," Lucy says in a low voice.

"I understand," I respond. "Choose someone you want to forgive."

"We got nothin' to lose," Judy says. Everyone nods.

In the next hour, I lead them through an empathy-building writing exercise (included in the **Your Turn!** section at the end of this chapter).

The last question is the most important. I give each one in our cleaning-closet circle a single sheet of paper with this prompt at the top:

I'm trying to understand a fuller truth about what happened that day.

Everyone writes, bent over their knees, including me, for about fifteen minutes.

"Okay, everybody, we're almost out of time. How'd that go?" I ask gently, as people start looking up and around.

"Whewwww," Shanille exhales. "This is tough. 'Cause I see my stepfather different that night he kicked me out. If I were him, I woulda kicked me out too."

"That's what I want us to look at," I say, looking around. "The first piece you wrote I told you to write from your anger, or write whatever you felt. The second, I asked you to use your pen as eyes, to see what you haven't seen before, maybe. To be like the Good Samaritan, the guy who actually saw the wounded man beside the road. To see the person you've resented and to try writing *toward* them instead of against them. How did you feel after writing the second piece?"

Lucy has been fidgeting this whole time, her leg shaking my chair. "This was big for me. I, uh . . . can I read mine?"

"Please," I nod at her.

She begins to read, her voice low but strong. She's too close for me to watch her face, but her hands shake as she holds her notebook in front of her. She's reading about something that happened when she was eighteen. It involves drugs, her mother's boyfriend, a fight, the boyfriend punching her in the face. Her mother ended up calling the police.

Lucy looks up at all of us and says, with half-closed eyes, "Being in here, this place"—she waves her hand to indicate the prison—"I've only thought of all the people I've hurt. People I hope will forgive me and all the s*** I've done. But people have hurt me, too. Like my mom. She had so many rotten relationships that put me through hell. But she was lonely. That's what I wrote about. I've been so mad at her."

"Forgiveness, Lucy. You gotta forgive yourself. Your mom might forgive you," says the red-headed woman.

"Can I read what I wrote?" Shanille asks. Her story is about her stepfather, who she's always hated, she said. She wrote about seeing him in the hospital, how weak and small he looked. She looks up after her last sentence and fixes me with her gaze. "Hey, I see him differently now, I do, but don't tell me I gotta go take care of him or do what he says. He's crazy. I'm done with him."

"I'm not telling you to do that, Shanille. You can forgive someone, let go of your hate, and see them with compassion, but forgiveness doesn't always mean reconciliation. Some people are too dangerous for that."

"That's right." All the women nod.

Judy, the woman with six kids, reads about her ex-husband, who didn't support them, and how she took to stealing to provide for her family. She closes by reading, "I made choices too. I ran him off. I ain't ever takin' him back, but I gotta quit blamin' him for everything."

Before the afternoon is done, every story has been shared. The first stories they wrote are the same stories they've written and lived for a long time. The second stories are new. The last words I heard just before I passed through the iron gate that locked behind me were, "We gotta do this more."

*   *   *

I've talked a lot about movement in the past chapters. If we want our writing to move our reader, it must move us first. The question is, where do we want to go? Maybe we want to stay as we are.

Maybe we're perfectly happy with our life and all that's happened and we just want to record who did what and when and maybe a bit of why and throw around a little blame to feel better. Maybe we don't mind a bit of anger and hurt. Maybe we've been estranged so long from a father or a sister that we don't really care anymore. But I'm hoping we want more. I'm hoping we've seen something of the force of words to enlarge our lives and the power of the Spirit to crack open our hearts and eyes. Don't we need them opened? I know I do. The hardest work of our lives, as daughters and sons, as husbands and wives, as human beings, is to tilt ourselves off our own hand-carved thrones. In my own myopia, I knew only one story: hurt daughter running from her abusive, emotionless father. My story mattered, but through words, through a seeking spirit, I discovered some of my father's story, which surely mattered as much as my own.

Are we courageous and daring enough now to write beyond ourselves toward the wounded others in our stories? I'm not asking anyone to whitewash sin. I'm not asking anyone to erase the past in a momentary spasm of feel-good forgetfulness. Rather, this is about using words to find, to write, to live out a loving-your-neighbor story, a story better than the one you've been living. Whether you include it with your life stories or not, I hope you say yes.

Through those two years with my father near the end of his life and the two years of writing after, I discovered it's never too late to embrace the ugliness of the past, to love even the people who ignored and harmed us, and to find the God who carried us through it.

Jeanna, who began the class writing rants against her ex-husbands, began new work. She began writing about her complicated relationship with her mother, her taciturn father, and her aunts. At the end of the year, in her smoke-and-whiskey voice,

Jeanna read her best piece from her new memoir: a story about her chain-smoking mother who grew potatoes in stacks of tires and her father who had been a miner and now spent most of the time in his rocking chair on the porch. It was a story that moved us all with its perception and compassion. At the end of the year, Jeanna wasn't the same woman who began the class.

Heather felt decades of hurt and resentment toward her mother-in-law shift and evaporate as she attended her deathbed—and then later as she wrote into those final moments.

Alysson, despite a shaky past with her family, discovered how much she valued her father.

Lucy, in prison that day, with a pen in her hand, took a first step toward her mother.

I'm not promising butterflies and hot-fudge sundaes at the end of all this. There is vast potential for healing and reconciliation through our writing, but there can also be a cost if we make that writing public. Whenever we're pursuing truth, especially about difficult relationships, someone will be unhappy. Anne Lamott solves this by saying, blithely, "All I actually have to offer as a writer, is my version of life. Every single thing that has happened to me is mine. As I've said a hundred times, if people wanted me to write more warmly about them, they should have behaved better."[2]

Yes, so many people should have behaved better, but they didn't and now what? We walk between the call to truth and the call to compassion: "Therefore each of you must put off falsehood and speak truthfully to your neighbor" and "Be kind and compassionate to one another, forgiving each other, just as in Christ God forgave you."[3]

Every writer must choose a path between the two. Here are some guidelines I've discovered along the way:

SIX KEYS TO WRITING ABOUT HARD PLACES AND DIFFICULT PEOPLE

1. First, write! Turn off the voices that demand you keep secrets and write into difficult places and relationships as freely and honestly as possible. Begin by writing for yourself only, not for publication. If there is trauma here, do this with a friend, pastor, or counselor.
2. Write in pursuit of truth, but never your truth alone. Write to discover the truths of other people's stories as well, even those who have caused you harm. Your story matters, and so does theirs. Humbly recognize that you'll never know *all* the truth about any one event or person.
3. Don't limit yourself to your own memories. Fact-check your information through research. For more personal stories, seek further information through interviews with relatives, neighbors, and experts. (Example: In writing about my father, I interviewed his brother and wife, consulted a mental-health professional, and researched mental illness.)
4. If you decide to publish, here are some recommendations to protect yourself and your subjects:

I'm not saying any of this is easy, but with these guidelines in place, you'll be surprised how relieving and cathartic it is to write with full honesty and yet also to grow in empathy as you write about hard places and people in your life.

What happens on the other end if you decide to make your writing public? Surely you'll be safe, writing from a desire for fairness and compassion. But even then, you need to know that someone still might get angry. Someone might call you, shouting, at all hours of the day and night over the lipstick they did or didn't wear, or they'll change their minds about being in your book after the book releases. They may say, "I never want to see you again" because you told the family secret, that you were once poor, or

  a. Change the names and identifying characteristics of people you're writing about to protect their privacy. (Let your readers know early on that you're doing this.)
  b. If you use real names, obtain their written permission to use their story. (Publishers will require this.)
  c. For particularly thorny stories and families, it may be best to label your story "fiction," allowing you to change as many details as you need but still capture the essence of the truths you want to communicate.

5. Remember, *all* the truth needn't be revealed *all* the time. Some events and stories cannot be fairly told until someone passes. Decide carefully *when* and *which pieces* of difficult events *can* be told. Then choose only those parts necessary to the story.

6. The final measure: If your writing is fair and compassionate and offers meaningful wisdom to others, then consider sharing it. Your authenticity can help others move past secrets and self-protective masks toward truth-telling and healing.

that you were once rich, or that you were hungry, or you weren't. There could be years of angry silence over something you *didn't* write. If there is significant family dysfunction already, know that your stories, however careful, true, and kind, will not change your family. But they will change you. And they will change those who read your words.

So it has been for me and for many others. We've all been given one life, one "wild and precious life," as Mary Oliver has so beautifully said.[4] Life has been granted to each one of us not to be hoarded but to be given away, fully, extravagantly. So keep writing. Tell the truth. Love your neighbor. Love your enemies. And keep writing.

I did. Four years later, that first story about my father led to a book about forgiveness that went out into the wide world. So many stories came back from fractured families, stories of fierce mercies and of unexpected restorations. These stories still come into my inbox every week.

Patricia Hampl, when talking about commemorating events in our lives, finishes with these words:

> I would like my writing to be precise enough, detailed enough so that the attention I bring to bear on something unlocks a door to the reader's life. In that way, by honoring one's own life, it's possible to extend empathy and compassion to others.[5]

For me, it began with one story written with trembling hands— one story about trying to understand another's story. Henry David Thoreau asks, "Could a greater miracle take place than for us to look through each other's eyes for an instant?"[6]

Through writing, we can make that miracle happen every day.

Your Turn!

1. This chapter is more personal than previous chapters. What thoughts and ideas made sense to you? What thoughts and ideas did you find challenging?

2. Read the two essays that follow: Heather's essay about her mother-in-law and an excerpt from that first essay I wrote about my father. Identify those places where we're truthful about our feelings and our experiences with a difficult relationship. Identify where we move toward understanding. Do these stories move you in a particular direction?

3. Now it's time to do your own writing! Here is the series of questions I used with the women in this chapter. Because the questions build on one another, it's best to do the whole series in one sitting. With a timekeeper, the entire exercise can be done in sixty minutes. Feel free to take longer if you have the time. Write freely, openly. This exercise is not for publication—it's for you!

Writing toward Compassion

1. Choose someone you're in conflict with or someone who has deeply disappointed you. Write down his/her name.

2. What lies between you and that person? Describe the break or gap in your relationship briefly but honestly. Don't be afraid to express the depth of your emotions.

3. Take five minutes to consider this person's life. Make a list of some major challenges, disappointments, and losses he/she has experienced. (Example: abandoned by father, lost jobs, raised by a single parent, mother an alcoholic, Iraq War vet).

4. Choose one of these events or circumstances that you know something about. In ten minutes, describe the hardship with as much detail as you can. Then write considering what kind of impact this might have had on his/her life and development.

5. Return to a moment of hurtful conflict between you and the other person. To write into that moment, choose one of the following options (whichever feels most appropriate). Take a bit more time with this, at least fifteen minutes.

   a. Write into this moment of conflict using this prompt: *For once, I want to tell a fuller truth about that night/day.* Write with a desire to understand this event from the other's perspective as well as your own.

b. If you'd like to take a step closer to this person and this event, try stepping into their shoes, writing about that event in the first person, taking on the voice of the other. (Example: I could write about one of the times my father left us. I would write as him: "I wasn't thinking about leaving until that last job. I knew I was going to be fired again. And so soon after losing the other one. I couldn't face my family again.") *Note: This is not an appropriate exercise for situations of abuse or other serious mistreatment.*

6. If appropriate, and if writers are willing, consider sharing your final stories in a LifeStory Circle. Giving our words and our out-loud voice to another's perspective can be particularly powerful.

LOVING AGAIN

by Heather Johnson

I sit by her side, stroking her thin, gray hair adorned with a rhinestone headband, a fitting crown for our family matriarch.

"She's close," the hospice nurse tells Todd and me as we hear the death rattle begin.

"How long?" I ask.

"Maybe ten minutes."

I wonder how Karen can be so certain. Then again, her job is helping people die. I stand and turn away from Avis's hospital bed, which is set in the center of her living room. Todd pulls me close as I cry softly so she won't hear.

"Maybe I shouldn't have come," I whisper to Todd. "Maybe she doesn't want me here. Maybe I'm causing her distress."

Todd remains calm, comforting. I should be the one comforting him, the second son of his dying mother.

Karen assures me. "I've been watching her. Whenever you stroke her head, she settles. Her breathing eases. She's glad you're here."

I want to believe Karen. But Karen doesn't know our history. In the beginning, Avis and I enjoyed a warm relationship. We walked often along Lake Michigan's shore, chatting about the grandkids before Todd and I adopted kids of our own. I even called her my "Naomi," after the biblical story.

Avis's idiosyncrasies were endearing at first, especially how she preached about her top three values: God, family, and country, although not necessarily in that order. In fact, I'm pretty sure Ronald Reagan ranked right up there with Jesus; next to the lighted Christmas star hanging year-round on the front of her carport was a white, metal sign with red letters declaring her territory: *Reagan Country.*

Avis also mixed God and country inside her house. Above the sofa in her living room, Avis displayed a framed photo of Ronnie wearing a cowboy hat. Next to him was a hooked rug of Jerusalem, and next to Jerusalem was a stuffed barracuda she caught off the coast of Florida so long ago that the fish had lost most of its teeth.

When it came to family matters, Avis knew best, and she made sure everyone knew it. She could not understand why other family members didn't agree with her.

We soon saw this side of Avis when Todd and I decided to homeschool our kids during their elementary years. We bought a travel trailer and took our books on the road. Sort of like living in a bookmobile, except we owned the bus and the books. After relentless coaxing on my part, Avis gave in and joined us.

The six of us traveled coast-to-coast and border-to-border on five trips from Williamsburg, Virginia, to Ronald Reagan's ranch in Santa Barbara. But our first trip to Texas should have been our last with Grandma Avis.

Avis felt free to critique our parenting, especially our requirement that the kids do schoolwork on our trips. (We were, after all, homeschooling!) One night, after another negative comment, I was exasperated. I stepped out of the trailer and marched over to Todd, who was stoking the campfire.

"I've had it with your mom!" I hissed. "If she doesn't stop criticizing our parenting, I might just have to break a commandment and strap her to the top of the trailer with bungee cords so we can get her home for a proper burial!"

I remembered Chevy Chase in *National Lampoon's Vacation* doing this to his infuriating aunt.

Todd's even temperament calmed my anger that night. But it was Scrabble that got us through our subsequent trips. Avis was the only one who could beat me, and she did so repeatedly, with outrageous words like *ZIT* placed over the triple-letter word square. We both had an equal love of the game that often redirected negativity and helped us focus on our enjoyable experience.

Through the years and the trips, I kept quiet about her criticisms of our parenting. Until a trip to Arizona to visit my dad with our three kids and without Todd.

One morning, while having coffee overlooking the contours of the Santa Rita Mountains, Avis began expressing her concerns about our kids again, all three of whom had been adopted from Russia. I had plenty of concerns myself. By this time, they had been tested by many specialists. Medications and multiple therapies had become our daily routine.

"You know, the only thing wrong with your kids is you," she blurted that morning over her coffee cup. "They spend too much time with you. They need to be in school to be socialized. This homeschooling isn't good for them."

I couldn't breathe. I felt hurt and anger running through me like flame set to a gasoline trail. As the kids' issues had become increasingly apparent, I was already plagued with self-doubt. Were Todd and I parenting them right and well, especially with their disabilities? What was it about me, specifically, that made me not good enough as their mother? Now, I felt sliced to the bone by the one I loved as my own mother.

I put my shaking coffee cup down on the table and looked her straight in the eyes.

"Avis, you don't know what you're talking about. Furthermore, your opinions about me and our kids aren't helpful. They're hurtful."

"Well, it's what I think," she retorted unapologetically.

"Maybe it might be better to keep your opinions to yourself unless I ask for them."

She glared at me. I stood up, walked inside to the bathroom, sat on the edge of the tub, and cried, my hands muffling my mouth so she wouldn't hear.

Avis's direct criticism of my parenting continued, spreading to extended family and some of my closest friends, who told me what she had said. I felt betrayed and began distancing myself from her, going to the lake less often, avoiding being in her presence without Todd. But in the last two years of her life, through her steady, rapid decline, I began feeling compassion for her. The early love we once shared began returning. After all, she was losing control of her family, her decisions, her bodily functions. How would I feel if I were in her position? What would I want in my last months?

I bought her fuzzy, fingerless gloves for her always-cold hands. I made her favorite apricot-shortbread cookies that always brought a smile to her face. I cleaned her house, and she not only allowed me, she thanked me.

I began seeing my part in our broken relationship, how my own insecurities allowed her critical words to take hold and fester. And I began recognizing that much of what she said and did came from fear of losing her family, whom she deeply loved, from fear of losing control.

Now, she had lost all control. She could do nothing but lie still as we swabbed the saliva she could no longer swallow, as we loved her the best we could.

In those final moments, her breath became shallow and soft. As I sat beside her on the bed, I saw the death of each of us. Now I wanted only one thing: I wanted Avis to pass peacefully, surrounded by love.

A few moments later, I place my hand on her arm. No response. No movement of her chest. I lower my ear. No rattle. No breath. Her eyes are frozen, half-opened.

"I think she's gone."

"No, she's still breathing," Todd says to me, hoping.

Karen rises from the old oak table where the family has gathered for decades and walks past Todd. She places the stethoscope's metal disk over Avis's heart. We wait in silence.

Karen gently removes the stethoscope and pulls them from her ears. Her next three words shatter my husband's wishful thinking.

"She's with God."

I hold Todd's hand, tighter than before. He squeezes mine.

His tears fall freely now. He leans over the bed and pulls the white blanket up to his mother's chin as if she needs to be warmed. Tenderly, he closes her half-open eyes with his fingers and kisses her forehead. Karen calls the funeral home. Within the hour, Avis's lifeless body is bagged and removed on a gurney. Later, her body would be cremated and her life memorialized.

Something else went out on that gurney the day of my mother-in-law's death. I saw it. My grievances and hurt were bagged and wheeled out with her. They would burn to ash like her lifeless body.

I know we'll be together again someday. And when we are, I can't wait to tell her she's still my Naomi. And then I'll say, "Let's get that Scrabble game. And this time, I get the *Z*."

FINDING OUR NAMES

by Leslie Leyland Fields

Fathers and teachers, I ponder, "What is hell?" I maintain that it is the suffering of being unable to love.
FYODOR DOSTOYEVSKY, *THE BROTHERS KARAMAZOV*

When my father dies, I may not know about it for days. The people at his housing complex in Sarasota, Florida, don't know that he has children—six, actually. He has not told anyone about this fact of his life. When he collapsed on the sidewalk last year, it was at least a week before I heard.

I am practicing now, writing about him, venturing out onto a vast empty plain, knowing that day is coming. He is eighty-six, I think, with diabetes, phlebitis, and smoker's lungs that heave his chest with every breath. We will not have a service. The cessation of his breath will not be enough to draw us together. No one would cry. I don't want to go to a funeral where no one cries.

When I was nine, I remember him standing in the den, his dark suit on, his hat, a gray overcoat, the clothes he wore when he drove off every day. A traveling salesman, like his father. But his jobs never lasted for long. He was always fired. My throat caught as he stood there, suitcase in hand. He was leaving: my first memory of his many banishments.

When I was in eighth grade, he left on his own. We had a little money left in the bank from the sale of our last house three years before—less than a thousand dollars. Our cupboards had always been sparse, but now we were down to twenty-seven dollars a week for food, eating canned mackerel for dinner, boiled chicken necks, or cracked eggs that we bought for twenty-five cents a dozen. On one of these days, my father drove to the bank, withdrew all that was left to fix his car, and then motored off. We found him one night, a month or two later, I think. I am not sure how long. He came back, promising that he would keep a job; he would show interest in his family; he would care about his children; he would be a husband and a father. I never wondered why he did not do any of these things.

He had been Christian Science for a while, then nothing, then an atheist, with special enthusiasm for UFOs. He watched for them every clear summer night, standing out on the grass, surveying the dark tent overhead. When we were younger, we watched, too, sometimes. He told us of spaceships he had seen, close-up, of fireballs shooting at him right there on our back road in New Hampshire— his conversion experience. He never wavered in his belief after that. Except one year. A letter with his tight scrawl showed up in my mailbox, the second or third letter he had ever written to me. He had read all the way through the New Testament, he wrote. He believed in Jesus. Would I forgive him? I cried bitterly for two days after that letter, because I could claim no part in his scandalous redemption. I had never even thought to pray for him. And I was not sure I could forgive him—for my persistent invisibility, the times he made me touch him while tucking me in at night, the poverty and the work. . . . A year later, after a flurry of mail between us, he wrote his last letter for a while, tucked inside a box of all the books I had sent him, along with magazines with aliens and spaceships on the covers: *Dear*

Leslie, don't call me daddy anymore. I am returning all the books you've sent, I don't have room for them on my boat. Don't talk to me about God or church. I'm sending you some magazines you should read.

Fifteen years later, we all flew down to Florida, my husband and children and I. This was my children's only chance to meet their grandfather. He was eighty-four then. They had little curiosity about him, and he knew nothing about them. I wanted them to know who he was for themselves. Someday they would care.

I warned the older kids, sixteen to nine years old, that he probably would not look at them or ask their names or ages. I didn't tell them he was their grandfather; I just told them this man was my father.

When we pulled up to the VA-housing complex in Sarasota, my husband, Duncan, who was driving, saw him first. "There he is."

I recognized his head, nearly bald, distinctively square, with a barely visible neck, dark-skinned. All as I remembered. But heavy, maybe forty pounds heavier than the last time I had seen him. He was wearing shorts and a jersey, the jersey tight over his belly. I stared at him, suddenly frozen. What do I do? How do I play this scene? Loving daughter greeting long-lost father? Kind daughter bringing her children to meet their invisible grandfather? The van stopped. I got out slowly. The side doors opened, and the kids piled out, one after another. My father stood there watching, looking past the kids, not seeming to see them. I suddenly knew what to do. I smiled and hugged him lightly, patting him on the back.

"Hi, how ahh ya?" he asked in his Massachusetts accent. He smiled a little, showing most of his teeth broken or gone.

"Good. We had a little trouble finding this place," I said, with false brightness.

He walked us around his apartment complex and then up to his room. "I cleaned up for you." He grimaced, waving around the room, showing us the results—a box of a room awash in old newspapers and stacks of magazines and ash trays, a bed and couch taking up most of the floor space. He showed me his refrigerator and the contents of his freezer—mostly cheap TV dinners and ice cream. My brother told me he had eaten ice cream before bed every night of his life since the divorce. Coffee in the morning, cigarettes, ice cream at night, UFOs. That was all he needed.

We loaded into the van, nine of us now, and drove to Crystal Beach on his suggestion. Everyone went in the water except my father and me. We sat there in the white sun on the white beach, just he and I. This was my last chance to know who he was, to find a fissure, something to take me down into that frozen stillness. I asked him about the war, about his mother and father, about his childhood—I knew so little. He didn't remember much and answered in short, vague sentences, spoken sideways, eyes always away. I was bothering him. I hadn't seen him for ten years, but all he wanted to do was sit in the sun, watch the water, and be quiet.

Two hours later, we were headed back, the day at the beach already exhausted. Had we really spent all that money to fly down here for these two hours? He hadn't asked the names of my children or spoken to them. We dropped him off at his building. I got out of the car to say good-bye, my body leaden, ready to drive away. I gave him a quick hug, shoulders only, not wanting to feel his body against mine. As I pulled away, he held on and looked me in the eyes, his face just a foot away from mine, and said, "You're amazing."

I startled, not believing what I had heard. "What do you mean?"

"Up there in Alaska, fishing, with six kids, writing. You're amazing. You're a success."

I blinked, aghast. He had thoughts about me? I patted his shoulder, pressed my lips into a smile, and ducked down into the car, quick, before I could want him to say anything more.

This is almost everything I know about my father. I had no

intention of ever writing about him, but an e-mail came last week from a friend whose father had died. She sent the essay she wrote for his service. It was beautiful and mournful, filled with all she would miss without him. Hours later, I began to write, and I could not stop. I wouldn't be satisfied with a pat and a fake smile this time. Not until a name was given—any name.

I began with a guess, searching on the Internet for information on schizophrenia. I read pages, scrolled through every personality disorder until I found it, from the American Psychological Association:

> A pervasive pattern of detachment from social relationships and a restricted range of expression of emotions in interpersonal settings, beginning by early adulthood and present in a variety of contexts, as indicated by four (or more) of the following:
>
> 1. Neither desires nor enjoys close relationships, including being part of a family.
>
> 2. Almost always chooses solitary activities.
>
> 4. Takes pleasure in few, if any, activities.
>
> 5. Lacks close friends or confidants other than first-degree relatives.
>
> 6. Appears indifferent to the praise or criticism of others.
>
> 7. Shows emotional coldness, detachment, or flattened affectivity.[7]

Why have I waited until I am nearly fifty to find this name—schizoid personality disorder?

I cried most of the week I wrote this essay, but in finding his name, I found my own true name, too: Mercy. Pema Chödrön has written, "How did I get so lucky to have my heart awakened to others and their suffering?"[8] What mercy is this, to be given life from one who cannot love or cry and to be granted the glad burden of others' sorrows? In *The Brothers Karamazov*, Father Zossima claims that hell is "the suffering of being unable to love." I am not sure this is true. I have lived in the house of such a man. His face is almost heavenly—content, his visage unwrinkled and untroubled even at eighty-six, a sure tranquility without the complication of remembrance or regret. And he has loved. It is never a question of not loving—it is only a question of what is loved. He loved what little he could.

Maybe I will go back when the call comes. Maybe I will go sooner. I could fly down and take him back to Crystal Beach. I wouldn't ask him questions or want anything from him. I would be grateful for that one moment when he saw me and almost spoke my name—

No, this is not enough. This is not the ending I can write or live. I have to want. I have to believe that fathers should love their children; I have to remember and write all that was done and lost and missed. And if, each time I remember, I can cry for him, for me, for my family, maybe this is love.

CHAPTER SEVEN

YOUR FOCUSED STORY
Editing

Every creative person, and I think probably every other person,
faces resistance when they are trying to create something good. . . .
The harder the resistance, the more important the task must be.

DONALD MILLER, *A MILLION MILES IN A THOUSAND YEARS*

"TEN MINUTES TO GET OUT THE DOOR!" I shout up the stairs, with a dish of applesauce in my hands. I'm feeding my nine-month-old son, Abraham, and throwing sandwiches into lunch bags, looking anxiously at my watch. The babysitter is late. Elisha, five, comes up beside me and thumps my leg. "You forgot to listen to me read last night, Mom. Can I read to you now?"

"Sure, go ahead. Even if I'm not here, I'm still listening."

Isaac, nine, yells, "Anyone seen my shoes?"

Noah, eleven, emerges from his room. "Sign my planner, Mom."

"Fred . . . gets . . . a . . . duck. Are you listening, Mom?"

"Freddy buys a dog, yes, go ahead," I call behind me as I retrieve the baby, who is stuck between the steps to the living room. His diaper is soaked through. I am trying not to look at all the toys on the floor, the dirt rimming the living-room rug. When will I have time to sweep? The sink is full of dirty dishes as well.

Naphtali, thirteen, runs down the stairs. "Don't forget I've got piano right after school, Mom. Please don't be late!"

I decide to skip the diaper change, run back for a look in the mirror, frown, pull another layer of red across my lips, head down the stairs, check the window—the babysitter is still not here. I scoop up Abraham on the way out the door. I see he still has food on his face.

"I don't have any shoes!" Isaac shouts at me as I speed past.

"Then go barefoot," I shoot back. He loses his shoes every day.

"This is it! I'm leaving!" I call. Baby in one arm, briefcase in the other, I stride, head down, into the rain toward the minivan just as the babysitter pulls into the driveway. I about-face, march Abraham over to her as the kids spill out of the house, then sprint back to the van. Isaac is running barefoot, shoes in hand, now diving into the open door of the car.

Within the next ten minutes, I deliver the kids to their two respective schools. At the first, the older three tumble out. "I forgot my lunch," Noah announces on his way out. Isaac is running for the front doors, dragging his coat in the mud. "Piano, Mom," Naphtali admonishes as she jumps out. Then one more stop at another school: kindergarten. Elisha springs out of the van and runs for the door while I blow him a kiss. We made it! And no one was late. I take a long, deep breath, then turn the car toward the college and hopefully, later, to my writing desk. I have lots of edits to do on the memoir.

Writing this scene now makes me sigh. Then laugh. Then say a prayer of thanks. Somehow, improbably, despite the whirling forces of kid energy and universal morning chaos, every school day we were able to collect ourselves into the van and end up at our necessary destinations. *Couldn't those six bundles of energy, desire, and excitement have gone quietly and gently into each good day, at least occasionally?* I would ask in a kind of prayer on particularly frenzied mornings. But I knew the answer: No. That would violate the norms of human behavior. And who wants docile robots for children, kids who merely do exactly what you say? (Yes, okay, some of us some of the time, but we'd totally miss out on the drama and stress that, in the end, grows our soul, etches interesting lines on our faces, and gives us harrowing stories to tell.)

Our memories have that same wild, unpredictable energy, don't they? They never behave, and that's a huge part of the mystery and the fun. The writing life itself is like this, as well. In composing this book, I have taken over two entire rooms in my house, with long tables littered with stacks of chapters and note cards. I have never written neatly. Perhaps because I've never lived neatly. And I think I'll be forgiven. You will be too.

I don't know what kind of life you're writing out of—whether you're overscheduled and frantic or serene and even-keeled. Yes, take care of your loved ones, always that, and don't worry if you leave the dishes in the sink as you write. Don't worry about dirt around the rug, dust on the blinds, and mud on your car. What you're doing now is important. At the End of Days, when we're whisked away to stand before the Judge, fiery, loving, and vast, I don't think God's thundering voice is going to say, "Well done, child. You've been good and faithful in cleaning your bathrooms, in washing your car, in keeping the dust bunnies under control. And good job cleaning behind your fridge all those years! Enter my heavenly gates—and here's your cleaning bucket!"

I think God cares about cleanliness and neatness sometimes, and so should we. But only sometimes. Writing is messy because spiritual work is messy. Over the last twenty-five years of writing books, I have learned this: If we begin a story and map out from the start with clean, straight lines where it will go and just how it will get there, and if we invest days and months, maybe years into this work; and if, when we are done, we end up with a book exactly like the one we first outlined the month or the year before—then we have failed. If we're lucky and we're doing it anywhere right, the story will shimmy and shake under our trembling hands. We will falter. Our perceived order of the world will shift. We'll get scratched and dirty. As our manuscript grows, so will we. And we'll be glad.

But how do we get there, to that gladness? How do we get the kids rounded up into the van and deposited safely at the school doors? What do we do with all those bodies spoken back to life? They weren't raised up to simply stand in that valley, vacant and lost.

This is the part of the dry bones story we often forget. The "vast army" is raised to its feet for a purpose. God said, "I will bring you back to the land of Israel . . . and I will settle you in your own land."[1]

Those risen bodies have somewhere in particular to go. And now, after WordSeeking into our memories and scenes, discovering a phrase, an idea, a paragraph that sizzles and pulls, we have discovered a direction for our own. And after writing into difficult places and relationships in our lives, we know where we want to go. We're not accounting for our entire lives; rather, the inner story helps us focus on a transformative event or a particular theme from a portion of our lives that we wish to excavate and name.

Michelle began her life story by writing about the onset of her dystonia, a crippling condition where her muscles spasm uncontrollably. But through WordSeeking, she found that the real inner story was her relationship with her mother and their shared affliction. (See "Of Bodies and Birds" on page 181). Now she wrote to further explore their common ground.

Jerry was writing an essay about his father. He seldom talked to Jerry on the phone, always passing it off to Jerry's mother when he called. While writing and reflecting, Jerry realized the root of his father's noncommunication: Jerry had advanced degrees and his father had only finished eighth grade. His father was self-conscious about his lack of education. Jerry edited and reshaped his essay. Now it was about his father's knowledge of the trees, of horticulture, of woodworking. His father *was* an educated man.

Amy Reiff started to write about a terrifying operation her son Stanley had when he was just five years old. She thought her story would be about fear, but WordSeeking led her in another direction. It was now going to be a story about strength and a surprising way she saw the presence of God.

Shall we do it then, unbolt the door and call her back in, our beloved inner editor, Mrs. Lynchpin? She may be a perfectionist who sometimes cramps our creativity, but when it comes to moving the bones and the bodies to their newly discovered destination, we need her.

In my own story, I needed her as well. In my last phone call with Kate, she asked why I didn't leave the island. What she meant was, Why didn't I leave my new life? Which also meant, Why didn't I leave my husband and new family?

But I knew now that my outer story wasn't enough. Because I did leave the island. Twice. I had begun writing about one escape—across the spit to the shack down the beach. But I knew now I had to write about another escape, about the time I got lost.

I had already written the outer story. And it was a good one, though possibly humiliating. I insisted on running a skiff on a day-long trip. Alone. On the ocean. In the winter. A snowstorm came up. I got lost, and the engine broke down, and . . . on the story went, eventually including the Coast Guard. In my defense, I was young and foolish, and I had been living for an entire winter on a remote island populated with two: my husband and me, building a house together, completely cut off from the rest of the world in our second year of marriage. (Don't imagine *Swiss Family Robinson*. It was more like *Cast Away* meets *The War of the Roses*.)

I wrote the scenes with lots of detail: how scared I was when it started snowing. When the engine died. When I knew I had drifted out onto the open ocean. When I thought I might die. But the inner story? I didn't know it yet. It was tempting to just stay with the outer story because it had woman-against-nature drama. It had storm, fire, and even some possible bears. What more could a story need? But I needed to know more than this.

I began to WordSeek into that day and it slowly came clear, word by word, what I was doing. I *was* escaping. I was escaping a place that wasn't mine: an ocean, an island, a life that belonged to my new husband and his family, but it didn't belong to me, and I didn't belong to it. It wasn't mine except by marriage, by proxy. My life was borrowed, shoehorned into what cracks I could fit in, like the tiny loft where we slept for three summers, that we climbed up a rickety ladder to reach.

As I wrote, as I did the WordSeeking into that day and all that happened, it slowly became clear. This event—more than any other—revealed the inner story of the whole book. I knew now this book would indeed be about endurance and perseverance. But something else came as well, something I didn't expect: I felt compassion for the young woman I was, and for my husband, for the two of us trying to make a marriage work on a wilderness island with endless nets, ocean, and fish we couldn't control. We knew so much about strength and determination and work, but we knew so little of love in those days.

But my fingers on the keyboard showed me yet more. There were so many rescues and second chances! I began to see that this was indeed a story of survival, but it was also a story of grace. Not easy grace. Hard grace, the kind you pray you'll survive. And there it was, the title and the paradox that came to shape the final story:

Surviving the Island of Grace. I knew then how I would shape the book and finish it. Kate would be glad for it.

It meant, though, chapter by chapter, I would do some outlining. I had gotten lost in my words and stories, which were now such a part of me I could no longer see them clearly. I needed a way out. I began outlining each chapter. Sometimes I would outline it after, descriptively, to see what I had written. Other times, I outlined prescriptively, ahead, deciding on the main ideas, the sequence of stories and support. Both helped me to see what belonged and what didn't.

This meant I had to let some pages go. (No! Not those hard-won words, those beautiful sentences! Not the story of the two pigs, Charlotte and Harold! And the goat—don't forget the goat! And how we got our Christmas tree from a boat that winter, hauling it home in a storm. What about trucking through Africa that next year? And not the story of my first octopus?) But yes. Of course there must be a letting go. Jacob had to let go that night. At some point, as the sun slipped above the horizon, Jacob released his stubborn grip on the man he couldn't defeat. It must have been a great relief. You can only wrestle for so long.

As the inner story came clear, and as my rough outlines made more and more sense, I heaved a massive sigh. I knew I had found the direction for my resurrected bones. As many other writers have quipped before me, it was now time to murder my darlings. But it didn't feel like murder. I didn't kill—I actually rescued them from the wrong story, saving them for the right story, whenever it came along. Those bones would come alive somewhere else. My story now was so much clearer, brighter, fuller, deeper without the distraction of the animal farm.

My own Mrs. Lynchpin rejoiced, even kicked up her heels. I had clear direction now. Every scene, every reflection I included would somehow illuminate the inner story, the story of finding and making a wilderness island my own. I wanted this for my readers. I wanted my readers to live my life wiser and better than I did the first time through.

Jeanna cut many pages, even chapters from her manuscript. Amy had to let some paragraphs go, the earlier versions of her story that she found no longer true. Michelle cut some pages about swamp and insect ventures. They were no longer part of the larger story, which was now a story about her mother, her dystonia, and her hope for restoration.

But you must understand: We're not editing our lives on the page to make ourselves look better. We cannot be the heroes of our own stories for so many reasons. If our stories are an undercover effort to hoist an equine statue in the public square with us, triumphant, astride, for all to applaud, it won't work. No one will read or care about our me-as-hero story unless we pay them. Nor are we being honest. If we make ourselves the unsullied protagonist, we're simply not telling the truth. Aren't we all made of dust, subject to temptation, prone to wander (don't you feel it?). We go to blockbuster movies to see superheroes vanquish evil, but we read memoir to hear *human* stories, stories that are nuanced, complex, and honest, where winning and losing cannot even be measured. But maybe this is the most compelling reason: We cannot be the heroes of our stories because these stories aren't actually about us. We're not studying our lives simply to know ourselves better (though this will happen). Or to offer up to the world our own guttural howl and yelp to the moon. (Though occasionally that is just what is needed.) We are not writing to justify or defend or ennoble ourselves. We are far more ambitious. We're after growth, however painful. We're after truth, however hard. We're hoping our words will serve others. If we're seekers, we may even be writing ourselves toward God, that he may further shape and author us, allowing us to find ourselves in his story and him in ours.

Not everyone understands this. Because we write our life stories in the first person, some people assume that we write out of ego. As I wrote day after day, I imagined my family of origin muttering, "Oh there she goes again, writing about herself. She's nothing special." The mutterings weren't imagined, actually, and they're perfectly right. I am no one special. I am everyman and everywoman, as common as dirt. I know that every quandary and question that plagues me visits a thousand, a hundred thousand others. So I dare to ask for all of us.

The memoir was one of those "dares." I didn't know it at the time, but writing into and through my first twenty years in that piece of Alaskan wilderness gave me a vocabulary to name this new life and world. It gave me courage to call out secrets and doubts. I finally saw what I was looking for all along: wholeness, belonging. At nineteen, I thought I found it in Duncan and in this raw, stormy land. But I discovered that what I was looking for couldn't be found in a person or in a place: It must be made, and it is made out of whatever is around you, whatever is given, whatever can be found. Sometimes all we're given is words. But words are more than enough.

In the next few months, the memoir was done. I was exhausted, but the bones were walking.

Maybe they were even dancing.

Your Turn!

1. Read Amy Reiff's short piece, "Held," and Duc Vu's longer piece, "A Bike after My Own Heart," which is set in Vietnam. Amy's piece is the final draft begun with the prompt *For once, I want to tell the truth about the night I was so scared.* Duc's is part of a memoir about his escape from

Vietnam. What kind of editing decisions do you think each writer had to make?

2. You've written scenes from your life, which detail the outer story. You've done WordSeeking into those scenes to find the inner story. Now we're ready for the inner story to edit and focus the outer story. To help you in this process, choose one of the life stories that you've brought this far. To prepare and help focus your thoughts for a new version, go through the form below, "From Bones to Moving Bodies: A Guide to Resuscitation," answering every question.

3. You're ready now to create a new, more finished draft of your story. But caution! Don't try to cut and paste a new draft from earlier versions. That's like putting a new patch on a tattered quilt. With your new ideas and insights, start fresh! Don't worry, all the writing you've done until now will make

FROM BONES TO MOVING BODIES: A GUIDE TO RESUSCITATION

1. What outer story are you telling right now?
2. What are some key moments and scenes in that story?
3. What are some of the insights you gained from WordSeeking into that event?
4. What is the one essential insight or "wisdom" you want to communicate to the reader?
5. What details or information from earlier drafts can be removed now to tighten and heighten the focus? What details or information needs to be added to heighten the focus?

Now, using scene, summary, and reflection, show us and tell us this particular story!

this new draft easier and quicker. Take as much or as little time as you want. With focused attention, and with your new skills, you can write a decent LifeStory in an hour. You can spend a year on it, as well. But the greatest danger in writing our stories is not that we write them too quickly—it's that we don't write them at all.

4. When you've finished the new LifeStory (which can be done in class), gather into your LifeStory Circles and share your work with one another. Talk about some of the editing decisions you made.

HELD
by Amy C. Reiff

It was in the middle of the winter, frigid cold, thirty-something below zero, Fairbanks, Alaska. The surgeon had told us that Stanley had to have this surgery: a bilateral derotation osteotomy with abductor releases. It could not wait; his hips were coming out of the sockets. Without this surgery, he would live in pain, deformed.

Stanley was only five. He had cerebral palsy. His frail body weighed all of forty pounds, held together by muscles so strong, his bones would not stay in their proper places. The muscles needed to be released to break the tension. If successful, the operation would bring growth and vitality to his body.

In the hospital now, it was hard to see him lying on a bed so large it swallowed his small, bent frame. My husband, Stan, and I walked with him to the double swinging doors at the end of the hall and handed him off to a waiting nurse. "We'll take good care of him. Don't worry; he's in good hands," she said, smiling pleasantly just before the doors swung behind the oversized gurney.

I felt weak. Too weak to face another monstrous surgery with Stanley. I was still healing from surgery myself. Baby number three, just four weeks earlier, had been surgically removed from my body.

I cannot lie—I was afraid. I was fearful of this whole process: cutting bones in half, removing a wedge of femur, legs rotated, plates attached, then screws drilled through. I was afraid he would not make it through. I was afraid of the pain he would experience; he did not have a voice or words to speak of it. I was afraid of not being able to console him.

In my anxiety, I prayed for God's help. Prayed that my body would be able to nurse my infant still. I wanted to turn away from this monster, but it seemed to keep coming. I think it was my mind that tormented me most. I wanted peace but just didn't understand how to let go. The muscle of fear was disjointing my trust. How could I trust deeply when I was hurting so deeply? I knew in my head that God was enough, but my body had chosen to focus on the needles, the scapula, the agony my child would endure.

How do you trust God when you are afraid? Can one really reach out and take it? This gift God meant it to be? Can one want it badly enough that the desire changes you?

As we waited, a group of us sat in a circle. Stan and I, our newborn, Rhett, our pastor and friends and my sister, Reba, all sat close together around the room, as if held in the hand of a warm and inviting personal friend. Reba, fourteen years my elder, had left her job to spend the next four weeks with us. I will never forget her sacrifice. They had all come to throw their arms around us, to encourage us, to pray and to wait with us so we didn't have to face these moments alone. They held us together with their strength, for our strength was gone.

When the nurses brought Stanley back, his face was white with pain. He could not speak to us to describe the shock of trauma his body was experiencing. It was all in his face—white, almost translucent. His eyes were sea green, their color lost. His small body was covered from his chest down in a fresh, thick white cast, with a bar between his knees. From the chest down, he was unable to move. Stanley lay still, frightened.

Here was our child, knit together by God from our flesh, known by our Father before he was even born. God knew Stanley now in this room of suffering. We knew God had not abandoned him. And neither would we.

We did not leave Stanley's bedside. But as we stood there, our son seemed too far away. Without warning, Stan lifted the rail that had come between him and his son. He bent his six-foot-one-inch frame onto Stanley's sterile hospital bed. With strong arms and love flowing through his veins, he scooped him into his arms, body cast and all, and held him. He held him through the tears of his broken body. Held him through the confusion of this nightmare. Held him through the rest of that day and through the night, until the pain gave way to rest.

Stanley was *held*.

A BIKE AFTER MY OWN HEART

by Duc Vu

When South Vietnam collapsed on April 30, 1975, my father lost his job with the US Air Force base in Bien Hoa military airport. There were seven of us in my family: my parents, second-oldest sister, next-older sister, younger brother, and youngest sister. My oldest and third-oldest sisters were married and had their own families. I was sixteen and would begin my junior year in the fall. We had no income whatsoever. My parents quietly started selling their valuables to get food. Wrinkles deepened around my mother's eyes, while my father's shoulders bent as if under a huge weight.

As the oldest son, who traditionally bore the main responsibility for the well-being of the family, I felt helpless and ashamed. Nobody in my family said anything to me because I wasn't eighteen yet, but the burden I felt was tangible.

My oldest sister's husband, Lam, was a captain in the South Vietnam army, so with six children, he was in a situation a lot worse than mine. Sharing the same familial humiliation, Lam and I often talked about what we might do to make some money. There was no possibility for a regular job because no one hired, and no one knew when the new government would begin closing all private businesses, as a Communist regime would surely do. Everything was up in the air. We knew that no matter what, some means of transportation was indispensable, however. Cars? Forget it—no one in the North owned any car, except the big-party bosses. Motor bicycles? Hardly. Very few folks owned them except the elite. Bicycles? Certainly—everyone could afford a bike. The VC soldiers and party cadres all cherished their China-made bikes as if the bikes were their beloved—cleaning them, polishing them, keeping them in their living room.

It wasn't possible to open a bike shop, but a bike-repair shop was not forbidden. New bikes couldn't be purchased, but new bike accessories were available for sale, especially tires. An idea flashed in my mind. I drove my brother-in-law's motorbike to the main flea market in Saigon to check the prices there. I was ecstatic at what I found.

In the 1970s, one particular type of bicycle was very popular, at least in Asia. The standard bicycle has a fifty-five-centimeter-diameter wheel, and a racing bike has a sixty-five-centimeter-diameter wheel. The Japanese produced bikes with forty-five- and thirty-five-centimeter-diameter wheels and called them minibikes, or simply minis. Unlike the standard frame with three pieces of steel tubes welded together, the miniframe consisted of one single tube bent into the shape of a check mark, similar to the Lexus logo. Their colors were usually bright and striking. But it was their round, black tires that caught my eyes.

As soon as I found out the price of a minitire in Saigon, I drove the motorbike to a repair shop in downtown Bien Hoa and bought every minitire there—about a dozen pairs. I tied them on the seat behind me. Not enough room. I put the rest down in a pile on the ground, stepped into the hole, pulled them up around my waist, and sat on the Kawasaki. Like a hula-hoop dancer with half a dozen hoops, I rode back to the flea market. They sold like hot cakes, and the merchants asked me for more. That trip alone earned me almost a hundred VN dong. I felt like a man.

From then on, my mission was to buy as many tires as I could find—not just minitires but all kinds of bicycle tires. I made my profits from the ignorance of the repair-shop owners. Once these tires were gone, they would never be restocked, for there was no importation whatsoever. And I felt great. When the tire supplies ran out—which didn't take long—I handled all main components: rims, hubs, chains, freewheels, chainwheels, pedals, brakes, and seats. Again, once their merchandise was sold, these shops would have no more parts as replacements for their clients, or they would have to pay much higher prices for the same items. Yet I never hesitated when I found a piece at low price. I had my own family to help support. The more the better. I expanded my territory to include Long Khanh and Vung Tau, two neighboring cities about one hundred kilometers away. I bought quick and sold fast.

But my business soon ended. By the summer of 1975, I hardly found any more profitable accessories. They all went to the flea market in Saigon, or the owners found out and kept them for themselves. But I had one consolation. I kept the best of what I had found to build my own bicycle: the hubs, chainwheel, pedals, tires, bottom brake axle, bell, and stem were French; freewheel and handlebar were German; chain, rims, brakes, spokes, and carrier were Japanese; the seat was Italian. I personally picked every item, and I put them together with care and devotion. It was a bike after my own heart.

When it was completely assembled, it stood there triumphant. The frame was in deep green with highlights in gold. The handlebar had a tall U-shape, preferred to the low bar for comfort and ease. The Italian seat was rare, for the Italians were famous for their racing bikes, not the regular ones. Its contours were so flexible as to snugly fit anyone. It looked good. It felt good.

On my first ride on the bike, I took a meandering route in the neighborhood. People noticed and chuckled. The pedals under my feet rotated effortlessly as if by their own will. Any bump on the road was absorbed by the springs under the seat. As I went once, twice, and thrice around the neighborhood with hands high on the handlebar, I felt confidence, pride, and pleasure. Every night, I kept the bike in the living room. Every day, I dusted it and checked the lubricants. The bike was the culmination of all the opportunities presented to me.

I adored it—but my next-door neighbors lusted for it. They were three young drug addicts who stayed inside their closed doors during the day and went out at night. They used to live with their wealthy parents but were kicked out because they stole every salable item in their parents' home. The parents bought the house next to mine just to keep them away. Thus, even though I kept my bike in the living room, I still locked it with a big chain.

One evening, my family had a prayer service for my grandfather. The bike was moved from the living room to the kitchen, which was detached from the main house. That night, the bike wasn't moved back into the living room but remained in the kitchen room overnight.

As soon as morning broke, I rushed to the kitchen—and

skidded to a stop. The bike was gone. I wanted to cry but couldn't. My insides were scooped out empty. The bike was more than a prized possession to me; it was part of me. For the first time, I understood loss. My gut feeling was that my neighbors had stolen it. (A decade later, these men admitted to stealing my bike.)

Lying awake late that night, I wondered if God had punished me for my business practices. The faces of the shop owners whose goods I had cleaned out stared at me. Of course, I didn't do anything illegal. But I did pretend to be in the bike-repair business so that I could buy parts more easily from them. And the way they looked at me when I returned to their shops to scour for more parts, they knew. Had the chickens come home to roost?

More than thirty years have passed, but I still miss the bike. It was uniquely mine, beautifully, wonderfully assembled. Even in the darkest pages of Vietnam's recent history, I could still find exquisite components to turn into something wondrous. Now, living in the United States, pastoring a large parish, I have much more of everything. But I find myself still doing it—creating and assembling shiny wonders after my own heart. Someday, I hope, I will stop.

CHAPTER EIGHT

YOUR STRUCTURED STORY
Ordering

*The artist goes back to the chaos and the ways in which it is experienced,
moment to moment through our senses, and pulls out bits and pieces of that
sensual experience. The artist gives it back to the reader reshaped. In selecting
and shaping and restructuring the sensual experience, the artist creates a vision
of order for the reader, not as an idea, not as a set of principles,
but as a kind of harmonic that's set up in the reader, a resonance.*

ROBERT OLEN BUTLER, IN *OF FICTION AND FAITH*

I SIT AT MY COMPUTER in my office, skimming the pages. This
is it. I look one last time at the introduction and the first chapter
and then scroll to the ending. I don't know if I can read these words
one more time. I try to imagine Kate reading these words, with her
critical eyes and pen. The pages scroll before my eyes: My niece's
near drowning, then the barnacles and the close . . . *Yes*, I sigh.
*That's it. The ending answers the beginning. And all the in-between,
the questions I've been asking for the last few months: Have I ordered
it well? Does the structure hold? Does it flow?* My stomach quivers,
my index finger hovers over the enter button, then answers for me.
I hit "attach file" and then "send."

I exhale, stand, grab a scarf and my trench coat, and tear out of
my office door. I know where I have to go. In five minutes, I'm at
Mill Bay Coffee, cradling a hazelnut latte and carving out spoon-
fuls of tiramisu made fresh that morning by Joel and Martine, the

French chefs whose pastries fed me through multiple drafts of a memoir I never thought I'd write, let alone finish. Even if no one wants it, I'm proud of the work I've done. I'm grateful for all I've learned, page by page, and the tiramisu is awfully good today, but what will Kate think?

I soon found out. Kate sent it out into the world immediately after receiving it. And then it began. A steady stream of rejections from the major New York publishers over the next two months. They came in the form of very polite letters (yes, actual paper letters!) mentioning the writing, the drama of the setting, but "the memoir craze will soon be over," they wrote, twenty years ago. (They were wrong.)

I took it in stride, sort of. I knew that rejections are the cornerstone of the writing life and that those who succeed are mostly those who persevere. My one comfort was my prescience over the rejections: "I knew no one would want a girl-in-fish-and-boots story." Maybe Kate wasn't such a hot agent after all.

But then there was a yes. From one of the "New York Big Ten" publishers. It was a hearty yes (and it was a double yes, including another book proposal I had shoehorned in: this a collection of dramatic stories from commercial-fishing men and women). Suddenly Kate was great, and she said I was too. My first memoir—and surely my last—would soon be in bookstores around the country. I quivered at the thought, then raced to the coffee shop again to celebrate.

Finally, the memoir story ends! And it's a happy ending! (Sort of. I'll tell the rest later.) Why am I starting this chapter with an ending? Because that's where we are in the writing right now. It's time to think about the three toughest chunks of our stories or our manuscripts: endings, beginnings, and the structure of the in-betweens.

You have stories on the page. You have scenes, the outer

story, and you've written into the inner story, knowing the truth is beyond, beneath, and within the events themselves. You've wrestled with memories and whoever has shown up to fight you for them. Then, after discovering that inner story, you've shaped and rewritten your piece or several pieces. You're seeing what to keep and what to let go. You've even written toward prickly people. Along the way, I hope you're sharing your stories with readers in one way or another. In all of this, you're experiencing the power of words to join and joint the bones of the past, to breathe air into those new-old bodies, and to march and saunter them into the present, with new beauty and wisdom to share.

At this point, it may be time to retrieve that four-letter word we shelved in the first chapter. Remember that scary word *book*? Some of you weren't cowed at all. You knew from the start you wanted to write a book, and you've borne with me through these pages with enormous patience. (Thank you!) And some of you, like me, quailed before even the thought of it (What? Me? Book?). But now you've got all these stories in hand, and maybe there's some kind of book here after all. Let's consider that possibility, perhaps even work toward it.

Whatever you're writing, whether it's a book or a sheaf of stories or even a single, long story, we're after order now, structure, putting this whole thing together. Even within a single story, there are often several moving parts. If you've created a sheaf of stories, how do you order them? Do you just start at the beginning, in the baby-blue nursery, and leap from one stake on the time line to the next, ending up at the funeral where your uncle Harvey and aunt Bertha stand next to the open casket, hats in hand, mumbling kind words about the dear departed while everyone eats fried chicken in the kitchen?

I started my first drafts of the memoir this way. Not cradle-to-grave, but that same measured march from the start to the finish.

But straight chronology has some pitfalls. I knew it as I read my story. And you'll know this the moment you pick up a story or a book that begins, "I was born in County Fair Hospital in Macon, Georgia, in 1932 and given the name Harvey Henry McHenry by my well-meaning parents. My first few years of life were blissfully happy, spent in our front yard with my sister and brother among the poppies by the picket fence."

There's a good chance you won't make it past the first chapter, unless Harvey is your grandfather and you know ahead of time that right out of high school, he landed in the infantry as a sniper in Korea, where he met with a tragedy that marked him for life. Then perhaps, with enough shots of caffeine, you would skim through the long, slow parts to get to the good parts. Straight chronology can trap us in a narrative that trudges a listless reader from "first this happened" to "then that happened, then this happened."

Most of us are not telling our stories for the history books or for the local museum, accounting for every bump, swerve, and trip along the long road of our lives—unless we have 500,000 Instagram followers, or we're in a reality-TV show, or we're historically interesting, which totally knocks me and probably most of you out of the running for a detailed biography or exhaustive autobiography. Your grandfather, though, may have led such a fascinating life that a straightforward account will do the trick. Go for it! Perhaps your life, too, can captivate us from beginning to end.

But remember, the real story we're after is the inner story. The inner story is not the record of everything that has happened to you; rather, it focuses on a key theme and transformative event in your life: the death of your mother and then how you dealt with your guilt and grief. Your spiritual journey from the Pentecostal church to Catholicism, exploring the theme of belief. Helping your son through rehab and what you learned about true hospitality. I originally thought my memoir would be a detailed account of my entire life up until then but soon realized the impossibility of that. Not to mention the cruelty that kind of blow-by-blow would inflict on my readers. The inner story—my search for home in a strange land—was more intense and focused, and like all inner stories, it couldn't be tied to a rigid time line.

Given the fluidity of the inner story, we're going to have to make decisions about the order of the events, about the structure of our piece. Right now, I imagine a few of you are miffed that I've waited until now to talk about structure. *Isn't that one of the first decisions we should make?* you're asking.

No, I respond politely. First you must know what *kind* of story you are writing. We don't choose a structure and externally impose it on our stories, especially when we're not even sure what our story *is* yet. We write into and under and around the whole thing until we know the outer story and the inner story. Until we know, really know, what we've come to say. Then we look for a way to gather the threads of the one story or the several stories and fit them together so they make sense, so they move the reader forward with insight and energy.

How do we do this? For that first memoir, I asked myself this question aloud in my little shed over the dock again and again, with a touch of hysteria and chest-beating. Where do I start? How do I finish? And how do I keep my reader with me through all the in-between? In my innocence, I had no idea I would have to ask this again for every book written thereafter. (You mean, there's no secret formula?)

Eventually, I decided to start at a turning point, as many memoirs do. I was wearily leaning out over the skiff in the middle of a long day of fishing. Days and nights blurred together as we worked the nets, week after week. Beside me, suddenly, a fin whale surfaced, black, serpent-like, sending a geyser of spray overhead, just a hundred feet away. I watched in awe. In my fatigue, I almost missed him. I wondered then, how much else I had missed that week, that month. What happened to that eager, fresh-faced, just-married girl who stepped off on the graveled beach of that Alaskan island just a few years before?

The moment immediately established the setting of the story and the tension that would drive the story forward. From there, my chronicle moved back and forth through time: forward into my life on this remote island, then a chapter that flashes back to my childhood, and all the surprising ways I was prepared for my Alaskan life. Then forward again a few more chapters through the early years here, and another flashback to events in my childhood. Like this, I zigzagged between past and present all the way to the finish line. The tension—would I survive this rugged new life and make it my home?—provided the energy to both hold the story together and propel the story forward, no matter the temporal switchbacks.

This is how we live, is it not? Time doesn't behave for any of us. Don't we know this already, how we fall from chronos time into kairos time at the mere whiff of Italian roast coffee, the memory of our grandmother hand grinding the beans she bought at Mr. Steiner's grocery?

And haven't we known since childhood that even if a story begins with "in the beginning" or "once upon a time" and ends with "happily ever after," anything can happen in between? Madeleine L'Engle imagined that time could "wrinkle." Einstein believed, "The distinction between past, present and future is only a stubbornly persistent illusion."[1] The week that I write this, the first image of a black hole appears on screens around the world, confirming what physicists have long speculated, that time moves in more than one direction.

In the biblical view, too, time is complicated, layered, mysterious. We are time-bound beings—but we believe we shall live forever. We are time-bound beings who can map the steps of our faith in time, on a neatly ordered time line, yet God knew us and chose us *before the world was even made.*[2] We are time-bound beings, but we can move back and forth from present to past to future through our memories and imaginations. We're instructed, in fact, to live in daily anticipation of the future, "when the times reach their fulfillment."[3]

Time is a playground, a web, a wave, a mystery. We may begin writing through the stories in our lives chronologically. Reconstructing the order of events often helps us understand how things happened, even why. But in our later drafts, we can free our narratives from a strict account of time. Not only because of time's own mischievous nature but, practically speaking, chronology alone is not enough of a force to propel our stories forward. We're looking for something else, something more. What is it?

At this point, the question is for our readers. Because this is not just for us, is it—all this writing, all this remembering? We write our stories for all that we gain ourselves in the writing, but are we not also desiring to "love [our] neighbor"[4]—that is, our reader—through our words?

For me, dear reader (whom I love), this means that I'll do my best to spare you the ugliness of my writing process. Over every early draft, I drool and cry. I snort-laugh, I smirk, I wail, I pray, and sometimes, I sulk. Those pages are smudged with mucus, saliva, coffee, and tears, as they should be. I don't want to pass *all* of this on. I want to pass on my most crafted stories about this strange and complicated world. I want to give you stories that will matter to *you* as well as to me. I want to give you stories with energy and force, that compel you to turn page after page. That might even change your life. Don't we all want this?

So, what will propel your reader through your story with interest? It's not difficult to find out. You're a reader: What do *you* want in a true-life story, in a memoir? (You'll have a chance to answer this when it's **Your Turn!**)

When I ask this in my writing classes, the responses are nearly always some version of these four qualities:

1. **A likable narrator.** ("If I'm going to follow a narrator around, he or she can't be a jerk." "I need to like her and care about her." "I need an honest, engaging voice.")
2. **Escape/entertainment.** ("I want sharp and vivid writing to sweep me off into the writer's experience." "I want a bit of escape. Like 'Beam me up, Scotty.'")
3. **To learn something** about human nature; about the life of faith; about a particular time or place. ("I want to finish the story knowing more than when I began." "I'm looking for inspiration.")
4. **A sense of unfolding discovery.** ("Don't give me predictability." "I want a sense of freshness and surprise that keeps me turning the pages.")

I'm going to assume, dear reader and writer, that you're likable. I'm going to assume your vivid scenes provide entertainment and immersion. I'm believing that your inner story, developed through WordSeeking and reflection, prompts learning and some kind of wisdom (without being too heavy-handed).

Which brings us to that fourth quality. How do we create a sense of unfolding discovery and surprise? As Robert Frost has said, "No tears in the writer, no tears in the reader. No surprise for the writer, no surprise for the reader."[5] One way to open possibilities and invite surprise is to play with time. Here's one way to juggle time.

We're back in my living room at Harvester Island. It's a gorgeous sunny day outside our room. The sun is spilling through the golden curtains. I can hear the rumble of a fishing boat as it passes. Twenty faces look at me, poised to write.

"So, here's what we're doing. I'm going to read a series of six prompts around a single theme. Here's our topic." I reach for a blue marker and write in cursive on the whiteboard:

For once, I want to tell the truth about when I lied.

I hear mild snickering behind me as I write the final word.

"Are we writing a confession?" Scott asks.

"It's good for the soul," someone quips.

Then Sue asks timidly, "What if we don't remember ever lying?"

We all turn to stare at her. She's blushing scarlet. "I mean, I just can't remember anything right now."

"All right, how about, *For once, I want to tell the truth about when I stole?*"

"Oh." Sue looks at the ceiling for a second, then nods her head, relieved.

"Choose whatever bad behavior you want for that last word: *lied, stole, ran away, cheated.* I'm going to give you one prompt at a time. After each one, just write for two to three minutes. This is WordSeeking, basically. We're after memory and ideas right now, not good writing. Ready?"

Half the class is poised over their laptops, the other half ready with notebooks and pens.

"Okay, here we go. What was the lie that you told?"

Twenty heads dip intently over their hands and computers. I wait until the movement slows and heads begin to rise. On we go, one question at a time:

- *What was the lie that you told?*
- *Where and when did you tell it?*
- *Why did you tell it?*
- *What's the first lie you remember telling?*

- *Name at least one lie someone told you that impacted you—for good or bad.*
- *Can you imagine a time in the future when you might need or want to tell a lie to your adult children?*

"Okay, is everyone done? How did it go?" I look around. "Sue?"

"I like the way this exercise covered memories of the past and then imagined the future. I wouldn't have thought to do that." Sue has been a fiction writer. This is her first foray into nonfiction.

"I thought of all the little white lies I tell every day," Tania offers. "Like, when someone asks me to do something, and I just kind of fudge on the reason I don't want to do it. I definitely surprised myself here. But what do I do with it?"

"I told about scratching my name into a desk at school and then lying about it," Amy says, with a lift of her eyebrows.

"I did two-for-one," Scott adds, his voice light. "I lied about stealing a Clark bar at the store when I was, like, ten. Man, I really caught heck for that."

We laugh. "What did you write about, Leslie?" Terri asks.

I'm glad she asked. I'm teaching this class, but I'm still a writer just like everyone else. "Okay, it's still kind of embarrassing." I sit down on the stool next to the whiteboard. "I wrote about lying to get into a movie theater. I had just turned twelve, but I only had one dollar. That was all my money in the world. And the sign said, 'Twelve and up: two dollars.' So I lied and said I was eleven. Guess what the movie was."

Everyone looks at me blankly.

"The movie that I lied to get into was"—I pause for drama—"*The Ten Commandments*."

We laugh. When we settle again, Scott raises a tentative hand.

"So, I'm confused. I've got a real mess here, Leslie. All these fragments," Scott says from the corner, looking worried.

"Don't worry. We're not done! So you've got six pieces, all of which are connected thematically, right? They're set in the past, in the present, and in the future, but they're all connected by the inner story, which has to do with lying. So experiment now with moving these pieces around to fashion a compelling story. You don't have to use all six pieces, but try to use at least three. Find a structure that works for your content. Remember, we're looking for a sense of learning and discovery. So, let's take about thirty minutes."

It's almost lunchtime, but everyone is absorbed in their story. At the end, each describes what they wrote and the structure they chose.

Amy wrote about a lie she told the principal in school. She used a straight time line, starting with her first lie, but she dipped into backstory and reflection along the way.

Tania wrote about all her little white lies. She started with the present, then flashed back to a memory, dipping into reflection, then ended with speculating about the future.

Gina alternated the past with the present throughout.

Sue created a bookend, beginning and ending in the present, but in the middle, focusing on a lie she told in the past.

Many structures are possible in every story we write. We have to decide what makes sense organically, given the content, and also creates energy to propel the story forward. Here's one simple means of discovery: Print out all your stories, or if you're working on a single story, print out the different sections singly. Then spread them out on a table and move them around. Try different sequences. What makes sense? How do your stories best fit and flow together? (I've done that even with the sections and pieces of this chapter, whose order and structure eluded me until the very last!) You might like the space between stories, wanting each one to shine separately. Or you can tweak the ending of one story and the beginning of another to create a smoother narrative arc.

After I've thrashed around for a while in various drafts and possibilities, when I'm ready for a ride out of the woods, I ask two questions of myself and this work:

1. *What do I want my stories to make happen in the world?*

   This question comes courtesy of Frederick Buechner, who reminds me of both the focus and purpose of each project and, more importantly, why I write in the first place:

   > Write about what you really care about. . . . Write about what truly matters to you—not just things to catch the eye of the world but things to touch the quick of the world the way they have touched you to the quick, which is why you are writing about them. Write not just with wit and eloquence and style and relevance but with passion. Then the things that your books make happen will be things worth happening— things that make people who read them a little more passionate themselves for their pains, by which I mean a little more alive, a little wiser, a little more beautiful, a little more open and understanding, in short a little more human.[6]

   Maybe this will be your question too. Granted, a writer never fully controls how her words and stories will stir the hearts of her reader, but without some sense of your own hope and desire, your stories are less likely to achieve them.

2. *What am I promising to my readers?*

   When we're stuck, when we lose our vision and energy, when we throw our pages under our bed and vow to fulfill our dream of becoming a lepidopterist or a surfing instructor instead of a writer, consider these calming words from novelist Morris West:

> You can't tell or show everything within the compass of a book. If you try to tell or show everything, your reader will die of boredom before the end of the first page. You must, therefore, ask yourself what is the core of the matter you wish to communicate to your reader? Having decided on the core of the matter, all that you tell him must relate to it and illustrate it more and more vividly.[7]

There it is. We've promised something to our readers (usually near the beginning of the story). The promise is directly connected to the inner story we're about to tell and our own purpose in telling it. All of that is what West is calling "the core of the matter." It's a touchstone for us as we write as well as a touchstone to our readers. It can be explicit or implicit. It can be a question or a statement, but it encapsulates the focus and purpose of your story:

- In the introduction to this book, I promised to help you discover your stories and communicate them with beauty and clarity.
- Heather hopes to expand her readers' understanding of faith, ability, and disability in her essays about raising three adopted children from Russia.
- Jana's memoir about her childhood and her unstable father explores the line between faith and delusion, helping people understand both better.
- My memoir is a story about an East Coast girl learning to find and make home in the wilderness, to illuminate ways we can all create "home."

- Stan and Amy, writing together, are sharing their son Stanley's story to offer hope and practical help to others with special-needs children.
- Jeanna's book about her childhood in the Deep South and her family memories presents an entertaining portrait of local history and family folklore.
- Vina explores the theme of family heritage and belonging in a story that braids her mother's decline into Alzheimer's with her father's memories of the Bataan Death March.

As you write, paragraph by page by chapter, let each word illustrate "the core of the matter" more and more vividly.

Are you ready, then? I feel the need for a sassy cheer to send you forth. This part of the process, the editing and revising, isn't for sissies. It can take a while. It's easy to get lost. And you know, it's okay to get lost. In every book and story I write, if I'm doing it well, I'm wandering in that dark wood for a while, not knowing the way out. It doesn't matter how many books I've written. Writing is always a walk of faith that requires long days and sore muscles and weary hands. Because what we're doing is immense and beautiful and significant. It's worth our time. Your story deserves the best words you can find.

At this point in the book, you know more than ever how much your story matters. I hope your breath still catches in your chest when you know again that the God who twirls galaxies and counts the cattle on a thousand hills still pursues a single sheep named you. Maybe you're beginning to believe it, that your story matters to *you*, that it matters to *others*—and that it matters to God. But maybe you are wondering if your *writing* matters to God. Or if you're not a God follower, if your writing matters to the world and spheres you inhabit. Your word choice, your sentences, the structure of your stories—does any of this matter on the grand scale? Isn't it enough to discover and then send out the truth of our lives?

I've been pointing to the path of truth since the start of these pages, but there's a hitch and a caution. Sometimes we so believe in the truth of our story, we take shortcuts in our writing. We hope the truth of our message will outshine the sloppiness of our work. We hope the truth of our message will redeem the artlessness of our art. I'm as guilty of this as anyone. I'm making a plea for beauty here.

But what about Mrs. Lynchpin and the steady campaign against perfectionism? you protest. *Aren't you changing your story here? Who can remember and write under that prickly, impossible mantle?*

Let me add one more layer to all that I've said before, because it is sweet and we need to remember: The universe is a multiverse of beauty, is it not? From the single-celled diatom to the trillions of galaxies beyond us, every shard is shot through with astonishing design. For the God seeker, we see not only God's great love for both beauty and truth, but the immense value he places on words. His own grand narrative, his redemption story could have been told through lists and dry histories. Instead, it comes to us through human authors who wrote God's truths in poem, proverb, parable, oratory, story, allegory, and debate, with words of force and elegance. The figurative language alone—metaphor, imagery, simile, allusion, symbolism—stuns us still. How does his story go?

In the beginning, let there be and there was; it was good, very good. Know that the Lord your God is one God, our Rock, our Shelter, slow to anger, of everlasting love, who spreads his table before me in the presence of mine enemies. My cup runneth over. And behold, she shall be with child and you are to call him Jesus, Prince of Peace. Whoever comes after me must take up his cross and follow, loving your neighbor as yourself, pouring out your life as a drink offering. Do not be troubled, my brothers. Not my will but thine on

earth be done. Well done, thou good and faithful servant;
happily ever after, even so, holy, holy, holy Lord Jesus, come.

In the midst of all this beauty and truth, doesn't our story deserve the truest, clearest, brightest words we can find? So take your time. Write fast sometimes, but also write slow. Don't short-cut across the field. Not all who wander slowly are lost. And understand, writing well does not mean you must clear your throat and write in a pretty-pitched voice. Don't change your voice on the page. Write in your own distinct voice, in your own words as the incomparable *you* you already are.

And now, this chapter nears the end, but I haven't finished what I promised: to say a word about endings. How do we end a story, a book (this chapter)? You must return to the core of your inner story and bring some measure of closure. In some stories, you're answering the question that lies at the heart of your quest. Most of life is too complex to answer with a straight yes or no. Don't be afraid of ambiguity. And trust your reader. Don't summarize or repeat something you've already said. End with a light hand.

But the most important thing I have to say about endings is not *how* to write the ending, but *when* to write the ending. Write the ending at the end. Write it last, after all the writing and revising of your story has done its holy work on you. In every project, I finish standing in a new field, a new valley, some place I could not even imagine when I began. In the forgiveness book, fists became open hands gesturing into an open-gated country. When I began the *Surviving* memoir, I did not even know what I was looking for. After years of writing, in the midst of roaring seas, doubts, the claustrophobia of an island with no escape, I found a place to land. I discovered life-saving truths to stand on—and to end with. And I hoped maybe others, stranded, could find a place as well:

I sat on a distant beach on our island one morning. I
was alone. I could hear the hum of a boat; two ravens
sat on a cliff above me, spatting. I waved them away and
could hear now the water licking its lips, and nothing
more. Then—what was that? A click, no, a popping.
It was all around me, a cricking and snapping as if the
beach were waking from sleep, pores opening, tongues
unsticking. I could see no movement, could not account
for it at all. I waited, my ears tracing the pattern to the
largest boulder on this part of the beach, about forty
feet away. It was blistered in colonies of barnacles and
mussels, blue mussels and thatched barnacles with
tall volcano-shaped cones that are yellowed and look
like fossilized teeth. I moved closer. I waited. There it
was again. A barnacle, the beak of the barnacle, like
a telescope in rotation was rounding the perimeter
of its own shell, ticking the edges as it went. Then,
scattered within my close range, I caught another tip,
the orbit of another maw, and another. Now adjusted
to these dimensions, the whole rock came alive with the
diminutive circuit of these beaks. . . . I was struck by
such vulnerability—no escape from attack. No escape
at all. Such obscene limitations! I almost smiled as I
understood. Here, halfway between land and water,
was the barnacle, a creature that literally grows its own
cliffed walls. His own form—given by God Himself—
entraps him; it is his prison, his island. But I saw: It is
also his mountain fortress, the very grace that sustains
his life.[8]

Those final words purchased a hold. Yes, it was a slippery
hold—but it was enough.

Your Turn!

1. What are some of the qualities that you look for in a life story? Make a list and discuss. Compare your list to the one in this chapter.

2. Read the two essays at the end of this chapter, "The Hands of Strangers" and "Of Bodies and Birds." Consider the beginnings. How do the writers capture your attention? Consider the endings. How did they bring closure? As a reader, were you satisfied—or not? What could you apply to your own beginnings and endings?

3. How did both writers structure their stories? Did they successfully sustain your interest and keep you moving through the essay?

4. It's your turn to do this fun writing exercise: Tell the truth about a lie! It can be done quickly, in as little as twenty minutes, or you can take your time. (Feel free to use the WordSeeking method here.)

    a. What was the lie that you told? (Or choose another iniquity: when you stole, cheated, hurt someone.)
    b. Where and when did you tell it?
    c. Why did you tell it?
    d. What's the first lie you remember telling?
    e. Name at least one lie that someone told you that impacted you—for good or bad.
    f. Can you imagine a time in the future when you might need or want to tell a lie to your adult children?

    Now choose at least three or four of these pieces and experiment with different structures. Time can be the organizing principle, but the inner story here, something about telling truth and lies, may need another kind of structure. Experiment by moving pieces around. This is your playground. Have fun!

THE HANDS OF STRANGERS

Joy Ng

Ronald McDonald sat upright on the wrought-iron bench just outside the front door. The primary colors splashed across his composite body shone in the sunshine. His painted smile belied the reality of this place we were to call home. My trembling finger pressed the doorbell. A kind, professional woman answered; she was expecting me. I didn't hear her introduction. Her words of welcome didn't register in my brain. I watched myself being escorted through the large automatic front doors of the Ronald McDonald House near Seattle Children's Hospital. The director herself was giving me the grand tour.

We began in the lobby. Nemo swam contentedly in a giant aquarium with his sea-creature friends, oblivious to the pain in the little faces that peered through the glass walls. The aqua-colored chairs were set in groupings, as if assuming residents and guests would pass the time in pleasant conversation. The counter at the reception desk held baskets heaped with treasures from well-meaning supporters, dropped off for the less fortunate children and their families who made their temporary home in this place. There were hand-knit hats to cover bald heads and beautifully decorated greeting cards, as if frazzled parents might have time to correspond with their now far-distant, normal lives. There were tickets to baseball games in the very best seats at Safeco Field and passes to the Woodland Park Zoo. When would Colin be able to go to a game or frolic at the zoo?

Miss Director continued the tour. The laundry room had twenty stacked, large-capacity washers and dryers, extra-strength laundry detergent, and bleach. Bleach and hand sanitizer were everywhere.

I watched myself follow her into the common kitchen. Everything was so clean. Teams of volunteers came often to clean. We would have our daily chores, too, Miss Director explained. Ours would be to clean the laundry room, empty the lint filters, wipe down the appliances, and sweep the floor.

"Here is the toy room, the movie room, the supply room, the playground. It is our goal to provide families with everything they need so they can give their full attention to their child," offered Miss Director. "Your room is right here, number 152." She opened the door and handed me the key. She clearly felt pleased and satisfied with the facility and support they were providing for needy, unfortunate people. Who were these poor people who needed help? Surely it wasn't me.

We were a happy, middle-class family. My husband, Jimmy, and I lived in Kodiak, Alaska, and all our children and grandchildren lived near us. Our two oldest girls were married, and we had five precious grandchildren. Our baby, Sarah, was eleven years old. She was the caboose, born when Suzanne was eighteen and Jenny was sixteen. We had just purchased a bigger boat, one that could hold all twelve of us at the same time! The grandkids were always at our house. The sign hanging in my ever-overflowing mudroom reflected the joy in our home, "Grandma's house; where cousins go to become friends." It was easy to say, "God is good." I liked my rose-colored glasses and the belief that we would all live happily ever after, together, on this beautiful island in the North Pacific.

Just a few days before, I had taken the children for a short walk to Spruce Cape for pictures. The abundant wildflowers were in full bloom—lupine, chocolate lilies, wild geraniums, Indian paintbrush, forget-me-nots, and fireweed. I carried two-and-a-half-year-old Colin. He didn't want to walk. He tried to smile for the pictures, but his smile was crooked and forlorn. He had an appetite. He didn't have a fever. He did have a lot of bruises, but what two-year-old doesn't have bruises? At dinner that evening, with a houseful of family and out-of-town guests around our table, Jenny wondered aloud, "Should I take him to the clinic?"

The next morning, Sarah and I went with Jimmy for a ride to the rocket-launch complex. We enjoyed the day walking from the command center to the recreation area. We cut through the brush to avoid the buffalos on the dirt road. On the beach, we looked for jewels, glass weathered smooth by Kodiak's rough surf. We were totally unconcerned, completely happy.

When Jimmy had finished his work, we began the hour-long drive back to town on the bumpy road along the rocky coast. We chatted about the wildflowers and the buffalos and our beach finds as the sun sparkled on the sea, lighting up the white mountains. There was hardly a cloud in the sky; it was a rare day in Kodiak.

Jimmy's cell phone interrupted our conversation. The message was short and sober, with no explanation. "Meet Jenny and Colin at the ER immediately." The rest of the ride to town was somber. No longer did the sun seem so bright. In the quiet of my heart, fear loomed. I cried out to God, but I had no words.

Jenny had taken Colin to the clinic that morning. A perceptive nurse practitioner had ordered a blood test because she didn't like his color. The unpleasant procedure completed, Jenny went on with her busy day, running errands and mothering three small children, until the hospital called.

We entered the tiny cubicle at the emergency room of

Providence Kodiak Island Medical Center. Colin, lying on the examination table, looked so little, so pale, so fragile. The glaring lights and stark-white walls were a sharp contrast to the warm earth tones of our happy home. Dr. Smith stepped into the room. I remember that he looked so very sad. He explained the results of the blood test to Jenny. She responded, "What could it be besides cancer?" He shook his head sadly, and a tear ran down his cheek. I remember that tear.

Suddenly, we were a cancer family. Colin's bones were full of leukemia. Jenny took my arm and pleaded, "Mom, don't leave me." I nodded.

Suzanne hurriedly packed our bags and met us at the airport. We left everything in her capable hands—our house guests, our responsibilities, our precious eleven-year-old daughter, Jenny's four-year-old son. I knew our friends and family were praying. I was thankful because I still didn't have the words.

The next few days are a blur of medevac flights, tests, procedures, pokes, and strangers. I stayed at Seattle Children's Hospital with Colin. The staff explained the protocol, the plan to attack the leukemia. Colin had a good chance of survival. A good *chance*? The treatment would last more than three years. Three *years*!

Now, I watched myself get the introductory tour. I was the poor lady who needed help. It seemed so foreign to me. Jimmy was in the business of solving problems and helping people. I was the wind beneath his wings. I was the one who knew the answers, met the needs, quoted the Scriptures. We didn't need anything. Everything had changed. My pride was shattered. I was broken, needy, fearful.

Actually, not everything had changed. God had not changed. Over the next three years, my perception of his goodness would change, though. I would learn that God's goodness doesn't depend on my circumstances. He would be there in the night when Colin cried in pain or raged from the steroids. He would be there when I was lonely and homesick for Sarah and Jimmy and the way things used to be. He would be there when new friends died, friends who had become so important and so close so quickly because of the cancer journey we shared. God would grow my faith and teach me how to humbly accept his help, even from the hands of strangers.

OF BODIES AND BIRDS

By Michelle Novak

I knelt in the swamp, mesmerized by the creature on the shrub. His strange contortions enthralled me: He was emerging from his exuvia—breaking out of his outer shell, undergoing the change from water-based nymph to fully adult dragonfly.

I watched for more than hour. It looked excruciating, bone cracking, the outer layer splitting along what we might call the spine. I understood entirely how this felt: It mirrored my own bone-cracking transformation to wholeness.

I had always been athletic and energetic. Even as I approached fifty, I still led a vigorous life and was untroubled at the thought of aging.

Until one day. Without warning, my neck swelled up, became hot to the touch, and my head fell over. My neck could not support my head. Afraid to move, I slept that way in a chair only to wake up the next morning with my head rammed hard onto the opposite shoulder, along with a spine-cracking sensation and pain I couldn't begin to describe.

My head never went back.

I was diagnosed with systemic dystonia, a complex neuromuscular disorder for which there is no cure and very little in the way of successful treatment. The dystonia affects almost every muscle in my body, with constant tormenting spasms in my neck muscles and surprise spasms everywhere else, twisting my spine, wringing it from top to bottom. It rapidly progressed, bringing with it a deep fatigue and a violent tremor in my hands and neck. I had no idea how much I'd be able to do, but I knew my active life was over.

What was possible for me in this new life, this new-old body? If this was how I was going to age, I at least wanted peace of mind in the midst of it. That meant I needed something to study. I've always been active both in body and mind. I love studying languages and have gained proficiency in several living and dead languages, which I use to translate ancient texts, particularly the Old and New Testaments. I knew if I was going to survive this dystonia, I needed a new mental challenge, but I could only study for short periods. I also desperately needed something to keep me moving. Even the little movement I could tolerate was crucial to keeping as healthy as I could.

One winter morning as I rummaged through my books, I happened upon my mom's old bird guide. The cover was gone, and it had seen much use. I smiled as I fingered through it, remembering the first time I picked it up as I visited my mother one sunny spring day.

We had been sitting together on the deck when two male hummingbirds appeared at the feeder. It looked as though they were fencing with one another. My mother described the drama she had been watching.

"Those two have been going at it all day," she said with a smile. Then, "Do you hear that song?"

My eyes followed her pointing finger. A shrub, under her description, slowly revealed the lovely song and impossibly red plumage of the male scarlet tanager.

"Later," she told me knowingly, "the heron will visit the pond for dinner."

Sure enough, a couple of hours later, we both marveled as a great blue heron made a gorgeous silent landing into her pond—just as she had said.

We looked at each other wide-eyed and giggled. I had never seen my mother like this: her mind vibrant, her sparkling eyes so fully invested in her place.

Her radiant joy remained in my memory as I closed the book.

Then I remembered something else: By then she, too, had developed a spastic rigidity in all her limbs and lost most of her ability to move about safely. But she was so rejuvenated when watching or talking about the birds.

I made a decision. I got a couple of feeders and put out some seeds. Soon the birds came—first the usuals, chickadees and titmice. And then woodpeckers, which fascinated me. By spring, I had an aviary that only an obsessive-compulsive, twisted central nervous system could dream up! The yard was full of new birdsong and vigorous life.

Most of my outdoor time now was spent slowly working through each feeder, moving, filling, and cleaning it. I experimented. I started talking to the birds, and they began to come closer, forgiving the twisted body and maybe even the twisted mind of one who talks to birds.

I learned to listen to the incredible arias of bird language, as they discuss, announce, and proclaim their intentions for their every movement and activity.

Many nights I study about them. And since my disease requires me to sit for hours at a time every day, I've learned to observe them in their own space through a disciplined, almost athletic stillness, a great accomplishment for someone whose muscles are still yanking, twitching, and spasming.

Now, every day a world of creatures alight in my flawed garden to be tended by a wracked body. I know what I look like. I move like someone twenty years older. But the creatures come. They stay. I'm charmed, and I feel deep affection for what I never noticed when I could see straight ahead.

When my head was permanently wrenched to the right by the unyielding spasming of many neck muscles, my eyes were recast. What was peripheral vision has become my central vision. Only a twisted body can know it and navigate the world by it.

The direction of my life has been realigned as well. I move sideways. I move slowly, with what might be seen as excruciating deliberation to those who only see straight ahead. But the best part is, I see small. I see slow. What I used to blow by in fast hikes, I now stop to examine, write about, photograph, and consider. That's how I met my dragonfly.

And my chickadee. At the end of May, as I was filling a chickadee feeder, talking as I worked, as was my custom, a chickadee landed on a branch just a few inches from me. He looked at me, his head as cocked to the side as the dystonia had tilted mine. I slowly raised my hand, asking in a soft voice, "Would you like a seed?"

In a moment, he flitted into my palm. I liked the soft pinch of his feet, and he seemed to like sinking into the flesh of my hand. We looked at one another with the same long, quizzical gaze. A few seconds later, he lit from my hand to the tree. He came because I held my hand out to the birds from January to almost June. In my old life, I would never have had the patience to wait and be still.

As it is with everyone whose soul is hidden in Christ, my brokenness has been redeemed, and I am whole. I'm twisted but whole. I know who I am: I am a helpless creature who must wait on the Lord for every good thing.

And he has cared for me in my new state and allowed me to care for others. I have a pair of robins nesting in my yard that come when I call them. I named them as Adam must have when things were new and slow. They wait for the food I give them. They drink and bathe in the water I pour out for them. They frolic and nest in the trees and grass I tend for them. I've finally learned why the birds made my mother so joyous, even in her pain and immobility.

And in these creatures, I see a new world coming when my body is made as whole as my soul. In that day, I will crawl out of my broken exuvia and stand erect to feed my chickadees with strong, steady hands.

CHAPTER NINE

YOUR SHARED STORY

Launching

Each of us is like a desert, and a literary work is like a cry from the desert, or like a pigeon let loose with a message in its claws, or like a bottle thrown into the sea. The point is: to be heard—even if by one single person.

FRANÇOIS MAURIAC, *GOD AND MAMMON*

IT'S THE LAST NIGHT of the writing workshop. We've just cleared dinner from the tables. We're circling our chairs, nabbing slices of chocolate cheesecake and sipping wine, settling in for the evening. I'm sitting between Amy and Zandree. I'm off the hook tonight. My teaching is over. This is their night, their reading.

"Okay, everyone, it's time!" I call out from my chair, still savoring the last bite of the chocolate crust. Everyone begins to settle in the living room, which has been our classroom this week. We've collapsed the tables and are now moving chairs to the perimeter of the pine-paneled room. While I'm waiting, my eyes follow the lines of the wood from the walls up to the cathedral ceiling. It was the wrong wood. We ordered eight-inch fir, but someone in Seattle sent us two bundles of four-inch pine, the kind of lumber used for trimming windows. It was winter, and we had to build this entire house in nine months. It would take two months to get the right wood shipped up. So we took it anyway. We loaded it in our two twenty-three-foot open boats and drove it back the seven ocean miles from the tiny remote village to our island. We wore five layers of clothing to keep warm in the winter ocean air, driving those skiffs heavy in the water with pieces of our new house. Then every board was loaded from the beach, up the long hill on our backs. I was eight months pregnant with my first child as I knelt to sand every board. Then I climbed the ten-foot scaffolding, hands over head, nailing up one piece after another, my belly heavy, until the whole room, days later, was done. I could not have imagined that this room, this house, would host so many more stories beyond my own.

Finally, the noise calms. Everyone is in a chair and looking at me.

"All right, everyone," I begin, my heart giving a skip. These are my favorite two hours of the whole week. "I've asked you to read something new, something you've written this week. Anyone want to start us off?" I meant it as a rhetorical question, ready to volunteer someone, but Stan's hand shoots up. It begins.

Stan starts with a miraculous story from his childhood in Guatemala. Then Sara reads about a difficult meeting with her brother, just back from treatment. Terri reads a terrifying scene when her husband threatened her and her children with a gun. Joan tells the story of her first encounter with God as a child in the Catholic church. Harry reads a story about a camping trip. Zandree wrestles with God as she struggles to serve malnourished children in West Africa. Amy is enrolled, reluctantly, in a charm school for girls in her remote Alaskan village. Vina shares a tender moment with her mother, who is battling Alzheimer's.

In that pine-paneled room on an island in Alaska, we traveled everywhere that night, into empathy, wonder, grief, fear, sadness, hilarity. I thought of Annie Dillard's famous words: "Why are we reading, if not in hope of beauty laid bare, life heightened and its deepest mystery probed?"[1]

The next day, as each one climbed into the floatplane, clutching a backpack full of one another's stories as well as their own, I knew that much more was ahead for them. Some would keep writing and compile a book. Some would start a story circle themselves. Some would take more classes. The end of the workshop was not the end; it was the beginning.

These are the best kind of endings, aren't they, that open into something more? My story with Kate ends like that too.

The reviews of *Surviving the Island of Grace* were mostly positive, but Kate and I were doomed. She didn't like my next book idea. In fact, she hated it.

After the memoir went out into the world, and then the collection of fishing stories, I took a break from writing to focus on my teaching and my family. But at forty-two, I was suddenly pregnant. At forty-four, it happened (impossibly) again. Over those two years, I found myself with not only two books in the oven but two babies as well. (Surprise! Surprise! And please refrain from clever quips like "Don't you know how that happens?")

I hadn't planned on being pregnant again, nor had I ever planned on writing a book about pregnancy. But I needed to. The years of writing the memoir had taught me the power of words to blaze a road through the wilderness into the past, and even to the future. I needed this now more than ever, for myself and for others.

I was writing this new story from my life with a fresh intensity, writing now to literally save lives: Many women in unplanned pregnancies end their pregnancies, I discovered. But one thing would be different in this book. I knew I had to write honestly from my faith, from my belief in God as the maker of every life and the loving designer of our days. What other hope did I have to offer?

I sent the first three chapters to Kate. Our conversation on the phone a month later went like this.

"Did you get my new book proposal?"

"Yes." Long silence. "It's not for us."

"I see." I knew she wouldn't like it. I take a breath. "Is it because it's faith based?"

"Of course. I can't sell any God stuff. You have to go to those religious houses. If that's what you want to write, you'll have to find another agent." Her voice was cold and dismissive.

And that was it.

Kate and I never spoke again. She was my agent for eight years, but we never became friends. I didn't mind. I never expected to have an agent. I never thought I'd actually write books. I couldn't dream that big. And I trusted that the end of that relationship would be the beginning of something more. (It was.) I believed I would find another agent. (I did.) That I would keep writing. (I did.) And I hoped that now I was free to write as explicitly from my faith as I wanted. (I was.) The ending with Kate was abrupt, but it led me exactly where I needed to go.

This chapter, too, must bring closure, and it's also a launch toward all that's next. Some of you are arriving here with bundles of stories, ready to go. Some of you may have read through the entire book first before going back and writing your stories. And a few of you have skimmed the first chapter and skipped to the last to see if you want to do this. (Just say yes!) However you've done it, here you are!

And now what should you do with these fresh stories, brimming with memory, heart, and wit, with fresh wisdom, these bones that have been joined joint to tendon, muscles strung, and skin, a "vast army" of stories now ready to go where you ask? Many of you are thinking of sending them out into the world. How should you do that? I'll sketch out some ideas about how to do this and then send you to a list of books that will tell you everything you need to know. But I'm here to share with you about the writing, mostly. I don't want this book to go the way of a conversation I had a few years ago.

Three of us sat together in a big-box bookstore. We were there to sign our newly released books. Between signing our books, we bent our heads together and talked with animation and complaint about all the tasks assigned to us as published writers, building our online "platform," starting a blog, Instagram, Facebook. We talked about marketing strategies, online promotions, the stress of following sales figures. We didn't speak for a minute about what bound us together, what we loved and cared for most: words and stories. I left the table that day empty and disappointed.

I don't want to end this book like that. But I've been urging you all along to write for more than yourself. So let me try to finish what I've started.

Here are five ideas for sending your words out into the world.

1. **Submit individual stories to magazines, journals, and blogs.** Some of the stories you've written and shared may have struck a deep chord with listeners. Consider shaping that story or stories into an article or piece for outlets that publish work on this topic or from this perspective. Read and research each outlet carefully, however, to see the length, style, and tone that best fits their audience. Most outlets have websites with writer's guidelines that outline their requirements. Send only your best work. But know going in that some publications receive a thousand times more submissions than they accept. (Less for blogs.) Rejection slips are the coin of the realm. No matter how experienced the writer, we all have an impressive collection of rejections. Don't take it personally. If you believe in your

work and others do, as well, keep sending off your work, but don't sit around waiting for a response. (It can take months.) Keep writing, keep honing, keep getting better.

2. **Gather your life stories into a single collection.** As you've written stories from your time line or your Artwalk, following the process from memory to final editing and shaping, you may now have a bundle of stories about significant moments in your life (or someone else's). They can remain separate stories, each one shining on its own, without a single narrative arc or "through line." This is the easiest, most efficient type of memoir to write. If you prefer a tighter book, gather the stories around a theme that will connect and unite the stories in some way. They can be arranged any way that makes intuitive sense, given the content and your audience. Even with family histories, however, beware of the pitfalls of the straight chronological approach, unless you write with wit, humor, and a compelling voice. An introduction will be especially important to set the stage, provide an overview, and create a framework for the stories that follow. Many of you will choose this option, and it's a good one. If you're writing to preserve your story or the history of someone close to you, know that your work is already a treasure—you have rescued the past from oblivion—and it will become increasingly precious as it's passed around the family and down the generations. *Dakota: A Spiritual Geography* is a good example of this kind of memoir.

3. **Create a traditional book-length memoir.** Many traditional memoirs contain a single narrative arc. This option is more time-consuming but is still the most common form of published memoir. Think of your stories as different

beads strung on a string. The string that organizes the stories is the inner story, the theme. Every story and chapter will enlarge, deepen, and advance the inner story/narrative arc. *Surviving the Island of Grace* follows this model. As you know from chapter 6, however, the story may move back and forth through time. Still, in comparison to a collection of stories, there is a clear sense of unity, cohesion, and momentum. In this form of memoir, story is king. While reflection is still a crucial element, let your story illuminate your "message."

4. **Christian Living Memoir.** I'm coining this phrase for a hybrid that blends key features of the memoir: the primacy of story together with the "felt needs" approach of Christian Living books. I used this approach in several books, including *Forgiving Our Fathers and Mothers*. Memoir—the story of reconnecting and reconciling with my father—anchors the book and provides the outer and inner story and narrative arc, but out of that experience, explicit guidance and instruction are given to the reader as well for their own forgiveness journeys. My friend Heather, a clinical psychologist, is currently writing about raising her adopted special-needs children, blending her story as a mother and providing her guidance as a mental-health professional. This option can truly combine the best of story and instruction.

5. **Start a targeted blog, website, or Facebook page.** Creating a book of any kind is a significant undertaking. Finding a traditional publisher for your work can be a lengthy, frustrating process. But with the Internet and social media, you have other options to use your material. If your life story centers around a particular issue that you've become

especially knowledgeable about (dealing with grief, the loss of a child or spouse, beating addiction, coping with illness, managing menopause, etc.) and you'd like to use your story and expertise to reach out to others, consider beginning a blog, a website, a Facebook page, or all three. They could serve as a ministry, as a support group, as an online story circle. Chronic Joy, a ministry for those dealing with chronic illness and lingering pain, sprang up from women who met at one of my writing workshops. They have a powerful, effective ministry that emerged from writing and sharing their own stories. They publish their own books, and manage a website and Facebook page. Be aware, however, of the personal cost and commitment this requires (as well as the possible liability).

But this list is far too short. My students and others have shown me how much more is possible as you write into your life. Here, I'll let them speak to you directly.

Writing and revising my autobiographical novel placed me into a deep peace that I haven't shaken. I also got an MFA, which opened the door to teach developmental composition at Northern Illinois University. I wondered how being called to write would allow me to help the poor. Well, the two came together, and I was privileged to work with students from some of the most notorious neighborhoods in Chicago for twenty years.
KATIE ANDRASKI

Writing my story not only gave me fresh eyes to see God in the difficult parts of my past, but continues to help me minister to others from hard places. My online ministry started through simply articulating those "treasures in darkness" kind of lessons on the blog. It has since grown into something I never could have imagined, teaching me God gives us our story for sacred reasons.

ARABAH JOY

I was almost forty when my life turned upside down. That began a wild, thirty-five-year journey of everything from learning how I'd been affected by childhood sexual abuse to earning a bachelor's degree at age fifty and a master's degree at age sixty. Even though I will be seventy-four next month, I still see clients for counseling. At the beginning of that journey, a speaker said, "Give God the pen and let him write your story." I believe the day will come when I finish my book for mothers whose children have been sexually abused.

MARILYN HEIN

After three years, I finally decided to write and share my story about my struggle with Crohn's disease. I got so low and felt so hopeless, I even tried to take my life. But I'm telling all that now, writing it and sharing it with my family. It's helped all of us heal.

"TIM"

When I write, it feels like a nine-hour prayer that leaves me with the peace I desperately need to keep PTSD at bay.

DONNA JAYNE SAMMONS-DEMOSS

Writing my life story, finding God throughout it, has been fascinating. It all started when I wrote about my first encounter with God. My goal now is to not just write my story but to help others write theirs so they can find the touch of God in their lives, as well.

JOAN MCPHERON

C. S. Lewis has a quote about friendship springing from the moment when one person says to another, "What? You too? I thought I was the only one."[2] Writing my stories has birthed many such friendships, as my willingness to tell my experience connected me with others who had previously felt alone in theirs.

MEGAN EVANS HILL

The biggest lie is that I am the only one who has experienced a particular thing. I've learned, in appropriate sharing of the hard and awful stuff I've experienced, that I am never the only one. Telling my story rebukes the shame that wants to cripple me and often brings freedom and sanctuary to a reader or listener—thanks be to God!

MICHELLE VAN LOON

Writing helped me to understand, to grieve, and finally, to celebrate the six years I lived in a remote, small village in Zambia. Writing gave me words to fill in the blanks and gaps of those hard years. To integrate them into my life story. Writing literally stopped my nightmares. Writing made me into an author, and I am profoundly, deeply grateful.

JILL KANDEL

Since the workshop, I'll have one essay published in a theology journal. What I learned about writing life stories has helped me write better sermons.

RANDY

I wrote *Under a Desert Sky* to discover for myself the faithfulness of God in the hard place of both parents having cancer. When I lived those years, I was so busy dealing with the Overwhelming Now that I wasn't always cognizant of God in the story. Only in writing did I relive the truth of his faithfulness. I now teach classes to other people touched by cancer and am a Voice of Hope with the American Cancer Society.

LYNNE HARTKE

But maybe you're not ready for any of this. Maybe your heart stopped at those words: *send your work into the world*. What? Send your private words, your most sacred moments out into the noisy, indifferent world, subject to critique and rejection? It was hard enough to share with your LifeStory Circle! And maybe you've worked your way through this book on your own, so you've not shared a word yet with anyone.

I understand the magnitude of this step. This is where I get hit hard too. Yes, I've been moved through writing. I've grown, stretched, learned empathy, listened to God. But now, let someone else read this? Share this with my family and friends? Publish a book? Even now, as I write this final chapter, though it is my twelfth book, I hear the same niggling at my very foundations: Does the world really need another story, another book?

It's a genuine question. More than a million new books are released every year in the US alone. Every time I walk into a Barnes and Noble, which carries literally a million titles on each store's shelves, I'm hit by a wave of inadequacy. Who needs to hear from me again? Surely countless writers over many generations have already said what I'm struggling to say, and they've said it more lyrically, more descriptively, more profoundly, more of every kind of adjective I can find for "better-than-mine." Does the world really need my story, *this* story?

I do have an answer. I've stilled my beating, doubting heart again and again by listening to Madeleine L'Engle's wise words:

> My husband is my most ruthless critic. . . . Sometimes
> he will say, "It's been said better before." Of course. It's
> all been said better before. If I thought I had to say it
> better than anyone else, I'd never start. Better or worse
> is immaterial. The thing is that it has to be said; by me;
> ontologically. We each have to say it, to say it in our own
> way. Not of our own *will*, but as it comes out through
> us. Good or bad, great or little: that isn't what human
> creation is about. It is that we have to try; to put it down
> in pigment, or words, or musical notations, or we die.[3]

Yes, we must write it, or we die, or some part of our memory or our family's memory dies. But this does not answer the question entirely. We need to write our stories, but does the world need our stories?

I experienced a deeper answer a few years ago. I was standing on a stage, a mic at my throat, facing a sober audience. Just a few days before, a man had pulled out twenty-three guns and shot into a crowd of twenty-two thousand. Fifty-nine were killed, hundreds more wounded. Most of us remember that day, though it blurs with so many other hostilities and attacks around the world that visit us on our screens each day.

This was a writing conference. Each person had come to learn and to be inspired. I had planned to say some of what I've written in this book: *Write your story for you, for your family. Write your story to name the world and give it back. Write your story to wrestle God. Write your stories to pass on the comfort you have received in all of your distress. Write your stories to attend to what God attends to. Write your story to pass on all you've seen and heard of the sacred in this world.*

All of this was still true. I believed every word. But that day, I wanted more. I wanted to hand out bulletproof vests instead of pens. I wanted to hand out shields and swords instead of speaking words into the air about writing words on the page. Never had I felt so shaken, so helpless. What good were all these words? Can words stop bullets and end violence?

But then I remembered that in his own violent world and time, Jesus didn't call out the military or teach self-defense classes or hand out swords, though all of this was warranted. Instead, he told a story. "A man was on his way from Jerusalem to Jericho . . . ," the same narrative the woman in the prison retold. About a man who was violently attacked, robbed, and left for dead. Who was then ignored, despite his need, by the very ones—a lawyer, a priest— who should have rescued him. The one man who stopped to bind his wounds and to nurse him to strength and health was a man Jesus' listeners despised. A man of the wrong lineage, the wrong ethnicity and religion.

Jesus just gave them that story. Maybe he used his hands and acted it out a little as he spoke, but he just gave them a story. Words that show us what it looks like to be blind, what it looks like to see beyond political and religious labels, what it looks like to be a neighbor, what it looks like to love.

So I did that too. I stood there and told that story, with a few changes: a Democrat passed by, a pastor passed by, a Republican passed by, but a liberal stopped and bound his wounds. Or a libertarian stopped and bound his wounds. I moved the labels around. I remembered that stories can do what guns and shields cannot: They can move us beyond affiliations, under the skin of our neighbors, even into the hearts of those we think are our enemies whom we are to love because they, too, are made in the image of God.[4] Every one of us—carrying the image of God.

But I couldn't stop with that parable. And I can't stop there now in these pages either. Because after that story we might think, *Okay, we need uplifting, hopeful stories that show love and mercy, where all turns out happy and well.* But do we know how hard that story was to hear? It rattled and shook up the entire social order. (Wait. The social outcast is the good guy? The super religious are the bad guys? We have to take care of strangers?)

Don't we know Jesus did this a lot? Every story he told was riveting, challenging, new. He valued people no one else valued: the lepers, the blind, the insane. He had deep friendships with women. He was scary in the breadth of his love and forgiveness. Sometimes in our comfort and security, we forget: The Good News he came to speak is not safe, not for anyone. The gospel's revolutionary message is not safe, but it is true. And it is beautiful, but it's a beauty that must cut to heal.

If we really want to offer healing to this cracked-up world, our stories must do as Jesus' stories did: tell the whole truth about this human existence. Yes, about its goodness and hope as well as its tragedy, absurdity, and folly. And like Jesus, we need to tell these stories with original words so our readers' ears and eyes will stay open and awake.

That means we need to be on Christian-ese alert. I catch myself all the time repeating truisms, using the same sanctified metaphors, the same theological terms that only a lifetime pew-sitter can follow. Even when my readers are kind enough to tag along, they're likely either yawning or too comfortably affirmed. Yes, I'm writing from a stance of faith, but I desire to write about this life with such honesty and insight that all people are invited in and find common ground.

To do this, we'll need to take our time. As we compose and

revise and finish our stories, may we do it with joy and patience. We don't have to be literary masters. I am not a literary master, but I labor like one. Resist our culture's twittering, constant instant messaging. Learn, practice, write and rewrite, study, pray, listen. Value your words and the story God is writing through your life. Take as long as you need. Do you know how long I spent on that first memoir? Eight years. I spend an average of two to three years on every book. I know I'm slow. But those words must wrestle me first. They must slay me, shape me, then raise me again. It has happened twelve times over now in every book I write, and I never want it to stop. If you want the truth of your words to live on the page, let them live in you first. If you want the truth of your stories to change hearts in the world, let them change your heart first.

What will happen then, when your words go out, near or far, to many or a few? Who can know what will happen? One summer, I roamed the hills and grass of our island in Alaska with a clutch of papers in my hands—a first draft of a book from a young woman in Canada. We wrote back and forth about her poetic words, about narrative arc, about story. Her words were piercingly beautiful, and I hoped she would garner a large readership, but who can guarantee such a thing? I had written seven books by then and knew the ropes. Solemnly, I prepared her for the reality of a first release, which often doesn't sell well. A year later, Ann Voskamp's *One Thousand Gifts* launched into the world, selling a million copies within the first two years.[5]

But fame and fortune are uncommon visitors for most of us. I know hundreds of writers, and only a few can claim even a passing visit with these handsome suitors whom we imagine are hovering around our doorbell, waiting for the moment our brilliant words take flight. I am not immune. I confess to occasional pangs of jealousy toward the twelve authors in the world selling a bazillion books. I think, in a temporary swoon, *How easy their writing lives must be!* But then I remember from my own modest shots of fame that every burst of attention brings greater responsibilities, not fewer. Another friend landed a spot on the *New York Times* bestseller list. His agent, readers, and global fan base now hold their collective breath for his next book. How can he write with so many others now to heed and please?

So enjoy the quiet. Your obscurity as a writer right now is a gift. Keep freely pursuing the truth of your life. Keep using "that one talent which is death to hide," as John Milton writes.[6] If you're doing any of this now, you're already famous.

Don't lose track of what this is all about. You may not have a lot of time to write. You may not publish. You may not end up on the *New York Times* bestseller list. None of this is needful. Because writing into our lives is bigger than this. If we pursue our stories, honestly and truly, they will send us on a pilgrimage that takes us, like Abraham, from one land to another, from a country of unknowing, through wastelands where the promise of a promised land appears invisible and impossible—but day by day, this journey moves us closer to clarity, to truth, to the very City of God, if we allow it. I don't want to lose out on any of that. I don't want you to either. And if in the whole course of your life you write one beautiful book, or five compelling life stories—thank you for sending out into the world the brightest, truest words you could find.

As you wrestle and write your story, joining joint to tendon to bone, I wish you leaps of joy, but also I wish you that crooked little sideways limp when a piece of writing is done and has done its work on you.

Let's go into the world limping together.

SEVEN "FEAR NOTS!" OF WRITING YOUR STORY

IN THE BIBLE, whenever God or his messengers showed up, in dazzling brilliance, to issue a task, a call, people fell down in terror. *Who, me?* So many times the divine response was, *Fear not!* Here, then, are the Seven "Fear Nots!" of Writing Your Story.

1. **Fear not! that your story doesn't matter.** It matters immensely to God, who is the author of your story. As the writer of your story, you're in charge of making it matter to your readers. Remember, we write not only for ourselves, to discover wisdom, truth, and beauty in the simplest and hardest moments of our lives, but we write for our readers as well, who are also on a faith journey.

2. **Fear not! that you have nothing "new" to contribute to the world.** Listen to Madeleine L'Engle: "My husband is my most ruthless critic. . . . Sometimes he will say, 'It's been said better before.' Of course. It's all been said better before. If I thought I had to say it better than anybody else, I'd never start. Better or worse is immaterial. The thing is that it has to be said; by me. . . . We each have to say it, to say it our own

way. . . . Good or bad, great or little: that isn't what human creation is about. It is that we have to try; to put it down in pigment, or words, or musical notes, or we die."

3. **Fear not! that you're not a good enough writer to accomplish your goal.** None of us is good enough to finish a project when we start. Some of us aren't even good enough to start! By the time we finish, though, we have become more than good enough. The struggle, the long hours, and the word-wrangling and prayer-wrestling will get you there day by day.

4. **Fear not! that you don't have enough time to write.** Of course you don't. No one does. But if you are serious about this calling and this project, you will find a way to reorder your life: stop watching TV, write while the kids are napping, get up two hours earlier than everyone else, take your manuscript with you on vacation. Yes, it costs you. Nothing of great value is free. Count the cost to everyone. Then, if you're still so moved, make room and carry on.

5. **Fear not! that you won't finish what you start.** The beauty of writing life stories is that every piece you write is a story saved from the Closet of the Forgotten. Don't let guilt or perfectionism steal the joy and wonder of whatever you're able to do.

6. **Fear not! that people will reject you when they hear your story.** I can make no promises about people's responses but know that most of us struggle with the same battles and afflictions. If the sharing of your experience offers meaningful wisdom and hope to others, then write it and tell it. Your courage and authenticity will help others move past masks toward truth-telling and healing.

7. **Fear not! that no one will read your work.** Someone *will* read your work. Maybe a few friends, your family, the ones you really care about; maybe thousands of strangers. No one knows this when they are writing, and it has nothing to do with the work. Just get on with the writing and editing, and trust that your life stories will find the people who need and cherish them the most.

RESOURCES

Selected Spiritual Memoirs

Barnes, Kim. *In the Wilderness: Coming of Age in Unknown Country.* New York: Anchor Books, 1997.

Adiele, Faith. *Meeting Faith: The Forest Journals of a Black Buddhist Nun.* New York: W. W. Norton and Company, 2005.

Armstrong, Karen. *The Spiral Staircase: My Climb Out of Darkness.* New York: Anchor Books, 2005.

Armstrong, Karen. *Through the Narrow Gate: A Memoir of Spiritual Discovery.* New York: St. Martin's Griffin, 2005.

Brown Taylor, Barbara. *Learning to Walk in the Dark.* New York: HarperOne, 2015.

Brown Taylor, Barbara. *Leaving Church: A Memoir of Faith.* San Francisco: HarperOne, 2007.

Buechner, Frederick. *The Sacred Journey: A Memoir of Early Days.* New York: HarperOne, 1991.

Buechner, Frederick. *Telling Secrets: A Memoir.* New York: HarperSanFrancisco, 2004.

Cairns, Scott. *Short Trip to the Edge: A Pilgrimage to Prayer.* Orleans, MA: Paraclete Press, 2016.

Dillard, Annie. *An American Childhood*. New York: Harper and Row, 1989.

Dillard, Annie, and Cort Conley, eds. *Modern American Memoirs*. New York: Harper Perennial, 1996.

Finneran, Kathleen. *The Tender Land: A Family Love Story*. Boston: Mariner, 2003.

Gallagher, Nora. *Things Seen and Unseen: A Year Lived in Faith*. New York: Vintage Books, 1999.

Haack, Margie L. *The Exact Place: A Memoir*. Murfreesboro, TN: Kalos Press, 2012.

Haines, Amber C. *Wild in the Hollow: On Chasing Desire and Finding the Broken Way Home*. Grand Rapids, MI: Revell, 2015.

Kurs, Katherine. *Searching for Your Soul: Writers of Many Faiths Share Their Personal Stories of Spiritual Discovery*. New York: Schocken Books, 1999.

Lamott, Anne. *Traveling Mercies: Some Thoughts on Faith*. New York: Anchor Books, 2000.

L'Engle, Madeleine. *The Crosswicks Journal: The Irrational Season, The Summer of the Great-Grandmother, and A Circle of Quiet*. New York: Harper Collins, 1988.

Lewis, C. S. *Surprised by Joy: The Shape of My Early Life*. New York: HarperOne, 2017.

Lynch, Thomas. *The Undertaking: Life Studies from the Dismal Trade*. New York: W.W. Norton, 2009.

Mairs, Nancy. *Ordinary Time: Cycles in Marriage, Faith, and Renewal*. Boston: Beacon, 1993.

Mandelker, Amy, and Elizabeth Powers, eds. *Pilgrim Souls: An Anthology of Spiritual Autobiographies*. New York: Touchstone, 1999.

Manning, Brennan. *All Is Grace: A Ragamuffin Memoir*. Colorado Springs: David C. Cook, 2015.

Manning, Martha. *Chasing Grace: Reflections of a Catholic Girl, Grown Up.* New York: HarperSanFrancisco, 1997.

Miller, Donald. *A Million Miles in a Thousand Years: What I Learned While Editing My Life.* Nashville: Thomas Nelson, 2011.

Norris, Kathleen. *Dakota: A Spiritual Geography.* New York: Ticknor & Fields, 1993.

Schwartz, Mimi. *Good Neighbors, Bad Times: Echoes of My Father's German Village.* Lincoln: University of Nebraska, 2009.

Winner, Lauren. *Still: Notes on a Mid-Faith Crisis.* New York: HarperOne, 2013.

Zaleski, Philip, ed. *The Best Spiritual Writing*, annual series.

Selected Books on Writing

Writer's Market (annual reference guide) by Writer's Digest Books

Christian Writers' Market Guide (annual reference guide) by Christian Writers Institute

Allender, Dan B. *To Be Told: God Invites You to Coauthor Your Future.* Colorado Springs: Waterbrook, 2006.

Chandler McEntyre, Marilyn. *Caring for Words in a Culture of Lies.* Grand Rapids, MI: Eerdmans, 2009.

Goldberg, Natalie. *Writing Down the Bones: Freeing the Writer Within.* Boulder, CO: Shambhala, 2016.

Hampl, Patricia, and Elaine Tyler May, eds. *Tell Me True: Memoir, History, and Writing a Life.* St. Paul, MN: Borealis Books, 2011.

Jacobs, Alan. *Looking Before and After: Testimony and the Christian Life.* Grand Rapids, MI: Eerdmans, 2008.

Lamott, Anne. *Bird by Bird: Some Instructions on Writing and Life*. New York: Anchor Books, 1995.

L'Engle, Madeleine. *Walking on Water: Reflections on Faith and Art*. New York: Convergent Books, 2016.

Lott, Bret. *Letters and Life: On Being a Writer, On Being a Christian*. Wheaton, IL: Crossway, 2013.

Marinella, Sandra. *The Story You Need to Tell: Writing to Heal from Trauma, Illness, or Loss*. Novato, CA: New World Library, 2017.

Roorbach, Bill with Kristen Keckler. *Writing Life Stories: How to Make Memories into Memoirs, Ideas into Essays and Life into Literature*, 2nd ed. Cincinnati: Writer's Digest Books, 2008.

Ryken, Leland. *The Christian Imagination: The Practice of Faith in Literature and Writing*. Colorado Springs: Shaw Books, 2002.

Zinsser, William. *Writing About Your Life: A Journey into the Past*. New York: Da Capo Press, 2005.

ACKNOWLEDGMENTS

Every book has a backstory. This one is different from my other books. It all started with a movie. Well, a video series: Your Story for His Glory, filmed by RightNow Media. Those good folks said yes to this crazy idea to come to Alaska to film the Harvester Island Wilderness Workshop, a writing workshop. Ann Voskamp was going to be there, alongside twenty-two writers. I knew the time would be especially rich—and it was. Thanks to their terrific efforts, we had a "movie," but where was the book? I hadn't thought that far ahead—but then, yes, of course there must be a book.

Since teaching my first writing class in 1984 at the University of Oregon, I have never stopped being astonished at the magic and wonder of the writing process. The only thing better than loving words, writing stories, discovering and passing on truths from this one life to another—is teaching others to do the same. Over these decades, it has been a deep honor and thrill to guide others in articulating their own life passages and then to witness the personal transformations that happened through it. But I know so many who cannot get to the workshops and classes, who ask, "How do I write my story?" So—this.

I do have an agenda beyond all this writing. Technology is isolating us, making us depressed and lonely. The process in this book is one answer, and this is my hope: to see people gathering around this book and video, discovering and sharing the extraordinary texts of their lives with one another. No communion is deeper and more healing.

This project all happened rather suddenly, so special thanks are in order. First, to Ann Voskamp, who took the first step of saying yes. Thank you for lending your inimitable voice and beautiful presence to this project. (And thank you for all you're doing in God's great world!) Warm thanks to RightNow Media (and Courtney and Caleb), who are so passionate about capturing and sharing words that bring life to the world. Shout-out to my agent, Greg Johnson, who's always cheering me on. And to all the good people at NavPress and Tyndale, especially publisher Don Pape, my editor Caitlyn Carlson, and marketing manager Robin Bermel. You're all so committed and wise, and you make me feel like family. Thank you!

Last, I want to thank everyone who has been in my classes, officially or otherwise, over the last thirty-some years. I remember many of you, thanks to the power of words and stories that turn students into lifelong friends. Keep finding, writing, and living the truth of your lives!

NOTES

INTRODUCTION

1. Samuel Taylor Coleridge, *Biographia Literaria* (Princeton, NJ: Princeton University Press, 1983), 6.

CHAPTER ONE: YOUR BIGGER STORY

1. Name has been changed.
2. Frederick Buechner, *Telling Secrets: A Memoir* (New York: HarperCollins, 1991), 30.
3. Frederick Buechner, *Secrets in the Dark: A Life in Sermons* (New York: HarperSanFrancisco, 2006), 137.
4. Patricia Hampl, *I Could Tell You Stories: Sojourns in the Land of Memory* (New York: W. W. Norton, 2000), 18.
5. *Fall of*: Matthew 10:29; *wandering of*: Matthew 18:12-14; *strand of*: Luke 21:18.

CHAPTER TWO: YOUR FULLER STORY

1. Deuteronomy 24:18, ESV. Emphasis added.
2. Exodus 10:2, NKJV.
3. Judges 8:34, RSV.
4. Dan Allender and Don Hudson, "Forgetting to Remember: How We Run from Our Stories," *Mars Hill Review* 8 (Summer 1997): 65.
5. James W. Pennebaker and Joshua M. Smyth, *Opening Up by Writing It Down: How Expressive Writing Improves Health and Eases Emotional Pain*, 3rd ed. (New York: Guilford, 2016), 10–11.
6. Patricia Hampl, *I Could Tell You Stories* (New York: W. W. Norton, 2000), 18.
7. Ecclesiastes 1:1.

8. Samson: Judges 16:28-30; Jonah: Jonah 4; Ananias and Sapphira: Acts 5:1-11; Stephen: Acts 7:54-60.

CHAPTER THREE: YOUR OUTER STORY

1. *Oxford English Dictionary*, (2012), s.v. "scene."
2. The Writing Cooperative, "What Is a Scene in a Novel?," July 14, 2018, https://writingcooperative.com/what-is-scene-in-a-novel-8f08df1dba94.
3. Census of Marine Life, "How Many Species on Earth? About 8.7 Million, New Estimate Says," ScienceDaily, August 24, 2011, https://www.sciencedaily.com/releases/2011/08/110823180459.htm.
4. "Origin of 'Kentucky,' State Symbols USA, accessed September 19, 2019, https://statesymbolsusa.org/symbol-official-item/kentucky/state-name-origin/origin-kentucky.
5. "Todd Name Meaning," Ancestry.com, accessed September 19, 2019, https://www.ancestry.com/name-origin?surname=todd.
6. Baltimore and Ohio Railroad.

CHAPTER FOUR: YOUR STORIES TOGETHER

1. Psalm 19:1-2, 4, ESV.
2. Luke 19:40, author's paraphrase.
3. To learn more, see https://www.facebook.com/galleytables/.
4. Romans 12:15, ESV.
5. Psalm 96:3, ESV.
6. 1 Corinthians 14:26, BSB.

CHAPTER FIVE: YOUR INNER STORY

1. Jacques Maritain, "Christian Art," from *Art and Scholasticism* in Leland Ryken, ed., *The Christian Imagination: The Practice of Faith in Literature and Writing* (Colorado Springs, CO: Shaw Books, 2002), 53–54, emphasis author's.

CHAPTER SIX: YOUR HEALING STORY

1. Patricia Hampl, "The Self that Can Render the World," interview by Mira Rosenthal at the 2006 Krakow Poetry Seminar, http://patriciahampl.com/about/interviews/.
2. Anne Lamott, "There's a whole chapter on perfectionism in *Bird by Bird*," Facebook, May 12, 2014, as quoted here: https://wordsfortheyear.com/2014/05/12/anne-lamott-on-perfectionism-people-pleasing-and-jiggly-thighs/.
3. Ephesians 4:25, 32.
4. Mary Oliver, "The Summer Day," *Devotions: The Selected Poems of Mary Oliver* (New York: Penguin Press, 2017), 316.
5. "Award-Winning Writer Patricia Hampl to Deliver Fairfield University's

4th Annual Catholicism and the Arts Lecture," Fairfield University (press release), October 9, 2009, https://www.fairfield.edu/news/press -releases/2009/october/awardwinning-writer-patricia-hampl-to-deliver -fairfield-universitys-4th-annual-catholicism-and-the-arts-lecture.html.

6. Henry David Thoreau, *Walden* (Edinburgh; Black & White Classics, 2014), 7.
7. American Psychiatric Association, *Diagnostic and Statistical Manual of Mental Disorders*, fifth ed. (Arlington, VA: American Psychiatric Association, 2013), 652–53.
8. As quoted in Ute Lawrence, *The Power of Trauma: Conquering Post Traumatic Stress Disorder* (Bloomington, IN: iUniverse Star, 2009), xv.

CHAPTER SEVEN: YOUR FOCUSED STORY

1. Ezekiel 37:12, 14.

CHAPTER EIGHT: YOUR STRUCTURED STORY

1. Written in a letter to the family of Michele Besso, as quoted in Dan Falk, "A Debate over the Physics of Time," Quanta Magazine, July 19, 2016, https://www.quantamagazine.org/a-debate-over-the-physics-of-time -20160719/.
2. Ephesians 1:4.
3. Ephesians 1:10.
4. Matthew 22:39.
5. From "The Figure a Poem Makes," Frost's preface to his 1939 collected poems; see https://www.poeticous.com/frost/the-figure-a-poem-makes.
6. Frederick Buechner, *The Clown in the Belfry: Writings on Faith and Fiction* (New York: HarperSanFrancisco, 1992), 78.
7. Quoted in Jon Winokur, comp. and ed., *Advice to Writers: A Compendium of Quotes, Anecdotes, and Writerly Wisdom from a Dazzling Array of Literary Lights* (New York: Vintage Books, 1999), 170.
8. Leslie Leyland Fields, *Surviving the Island of Grace* (New York: Thomas Dunne, 2002), 329–30.

CHAPTER NINE: YOUR SHARED STORY

1. Annie Dillard, *The Writing Life* (New York: Harper Perennial, 1990), 72.
2. C. S. Lewis, *The Four Loves* (New York: Harcourt Brace, 1988), 65.
3. Madeleine L'Engle, *A Circle of Quiet* (New York: HarperSanFrancisco, 1992), Section 1.9.
4. Genesis 1:27.
5. Ann Voskamp, *One Thousand Gifts: A Dare to Live Fully Right Where You Are* (Grand Rapids, MI: Zondervan, 2010).
6. John Milton, "When I Consider How My Light Is Spent," https://poets .org/poem/when-i-consider-how-my-light-is-spent.

EXPERIENCE YOUR STORY FOR GOD'S GLORY

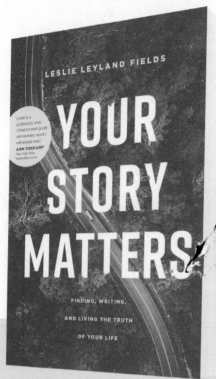

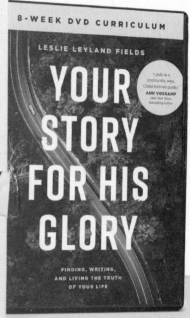

Read *Your Story Matters* together with the eight-session companion DVD curriculum *Your Story for His Glory*. Leslie Leyland Fields invites you to her Alaskan writing retreat to explore this dynamic process with Ann Voskamp and twenty other writers. You'll soon be writing from your own life, discovering new spiritual truths, reclaiming the past, sharing hope, and passing on your own extraordinary legacy.

Great for group or personal use.